The Working Bassist

What You Really Need to Know to Survive in New York City

The Working Bassist

What You Really Need to Know to Survive in New York City

*Includes over 30 interviews with NYC's top bassists!

JOHN CAREY

Planet Bass, NYC
New York, NY

© 2008 John Carey

All rights reserved. No part of this book covered by copyrights hereon may be reproduced or copied in any manner whatsoever without written permission, except in the case of brief quotations embodied in articles and reviews. For information contact the publisher. Paperback released 2008.

Editor: John Carey
Cover Layout and Cover Photo: Dan Taylor, dantaylormedia.com

Library of Congress Copyright Information:
Carey, John, 1975-
The Working Bassist, What You Really Need to Know to Survive in New York City
Registration Number and Date: TXu001581195 / 2008-07-19

Library of Congress Control Number: 2008938575

ISBN 978-0-615-22535-7

Printed in the United States of America

First Edition

Published by:
Planet Bass, NYC
Tompkins Square P.O.
PO Box 20556
New York, NY 10009-0556

For more information, visit www.PlanetBassNYC.com

This book is dedicated to my daughter, **Dylan Brooke Carey**, who provides me with the necessary grounding and inspiration that I require everyday.

Contents

Acknowledgments iii

About the Author v

Preface 1

Introduction 3

Interviews 7

Johannes Weidenmueller 9

Jack Daley 15

Patrick Pfeiffer 19

Neil Jason 24

Tim Lefebvre 28

Conrad Korsch 32

Mark Plati 37

Steve Jenkins 41

Jerry McDonald 45

Chris Tarry 49

Bailey Gee 53

Brian Killeen 57

Mike Visceglia 61

Roger Sadowsky 64

Irio O'Farrill 68

Meshell Ndegéocello 71

John Abbey 74

Malcolm Gold 78

Reggie Washington 81

Janek Gwizdala 88

Ivan "Funkboy" Bodley 93

Li'nard 97

Paul Frazier 100

Frank Gravis 104

Roy De Jesus 107

Jeff Allen 110

Kim Clarke 113

Percy Jones 117

Nicholas D'Amato 122

Dave Hofstra 126

Leo Traversa 128

Richard Hammond 132

John Conte 136

25 Tips for Success 145

New York City Wisdom, Perspective and Inspiration 149

Your Notes . . . 153

Acknowledgments

A special thanks to all of the bassists who were kind enough to take part in these interviews. Your honesty and thoughtful responses will assist in the decision making process for many bassists who are considering finding work in New York. Thanks to thank my wife for her support and encouragement while navigating through the New York City scene as a working bassist. I would like to thank bassist Mike Visceglia for the invaluable information he has provided me with throughout the past several years. Mike's creation of the "NYC Bass Brunch" gathers roughly once a month at The Rodeo Bar, NYC, and consists of many of today's top bassists in the NYC area. Each gathering has strengthened the bass community and has provided a collegial environment for working bassists, young and old, to get together, exchange musical ideas, "talk bass" and have some pretty amazing Tex-Mex food as well! Thanks to Chris Jisi for his suggestions and overall support throughout the process of writing this book. I would also like to thank bassist Roy De Jesus for creating the musical inspiration necessary to spark a young mind.

About the Author

John Carey is a professional bassist, producer, singer-songwriter and music educator living in New York City. He is a graduate of Stony Brook University, with a degree in English Literature and Philosophy.

John began his music career at an early age, performing regularly at well known clubs in NYC since the age of sixteen. His bass playing, singing and song-writing abilities have lead him to perform, tour and record with bands and artists of all genres, including rock, folk, funk, R&B, blues, fusion and world music. John is recognized as one of the few bassists who can fit into nearly any musical situation, providing solid, song-oriented grooves, whether playing bass in a small club in NYC, out on the road or in the recording studio.

As a solo artist, John has produced two of his own CDs. His first release, John Carey, *undefined psycho-chromatic G.R.I.D.* (2005, Planet Bass, NYC) explores the avant-garde. This completely live and improvisational album captures the stream of conscious thought processes between some of today's most talented, unique and interesting musicians. The CD spans multiple genres of music, and provides for a multimedia and multi-sensory experience. It is a truly fascinating record with an all-star lineup.

His second release, John Carey, *CL* (2007, Planet Bass, NYC), includes his original singer-songwriter/pop songs. In addition to playing bass, you'll hear John singing and playing acoustic guitar throughout the CD. His music is reminiscent of Sheryl Crow and The Steve Miller Band.

John is one of the leading bass instructors in New York City, teaching privately out of his Midtown studio. He has also recently taken on the role of producer for several NYC artists.

John is endorsed by Sadowsky Guitars, NYC, Lakland basses, Euphonic Audio bass amplifiers and speaker cabinets and Rotosound bass strings. For more information about John Carey, please visit www.JohnCarey.net and www.PlanetBassNYC.com.

Preface

The Working Bassist, What You Really Need to Know to Survive in New York City, is designed to inform bassists (and all musicians) interested in coming to New York City to pursue their musical endeavors. In addition to being informative, the series of interviews has been geared towards inspiring those who are already working musicians.

It was my goal to illustrate as accurately as possible what it's all about to live in NYC and to get work here as a bassist. I've tried, at all costs, to eliminate the "fluff" often found in typical interviews, instead focusing on what the music business is like in its current state and how it has changed over the years, specifically concerning bass related work in NYC.

Interviews include bassists who work as sidemen for high profile artists and bands, Broadway bassists, solo bassists, bass instructors, session players and even the great guitar and bass builder, Roger Sadowsky. All of the players interviewed work in NYC. I've selected bassists from several genres of music, upright and electric players, all ages . . . all professional bassists. Interviews were conducted via email, and have been placed in the order that they were received. Some of the players interviewed you may know and some of them you may not. *All* of them have been able to survive in NYC as working bass players. Their experiences within the "industry" are priceless for those entering the field, and their stories will continue to inspire those of us who are working musicians from around the globe.

In short, these interviews will provide you with an idea of what the music business is like in NYC from a working bassist's perspective. Whether you are considering relocating to NYC to pursue a career in music, or you're simply a music lover interested in learning more about the music scene in New York, this book will prove to be a great resource to you. Buckle your seat belts and enjoy the ride . . . This is what you *really* need to know to survive in New York City as a working bassist!

Introduction

When I first entered the New York City music scene as a bassist, I was sixteen years old and working primarily with only one band. The group had a number of gigs, and I had the privilege of playing many of the NYC venues. In the early and mid 90s, I was performing at clubs like Brownies, The Wetlands, Mercury Lounge, The Bitter End and The China Club on a regular basis. I was also fortunate that the singer-songwriter was a great musician and hired some of the best talent in town for all of his shows and recordings. I had the opportunity to play and record with such great musicians as Steve Holley, Dave Eggar, Doug Petty, John Abbey and Frank Bellucci to name a few, all before the age of nineteen. Working with older, established and better musicians enabled me to grow as a player and to network as well.

As a teen I received an early education, learning what it meant to be a working player in NYC. Gig after gig, I began to hone in on the craft of creating basslines that supported the song. It's also worth mentioning that I was living on my own from this age; having to make rent early on while aspiring to be a bassist made me strive even harder at making connections and getting gigs . . . I didn't have any room for failure. From these experiences, I developed the skills and confidence necessary to branch out, work with many other artists and musicians, and earn a living as a bassist in New York.

Other than being young, willing to take on a lot of work and being mature enough to provide basslines that supported the song, I discovered that playing other instruments gave me an advantage over musicians who *only* played bass. And beyond musical abilities, having good organizational and business skills were also a reason why I remained working. Basic business skills are almost equally important as one's music abilities. Remember, it's the music *business* you are attempting to be a part of. You need to make others aware of who you are and what you can offer as a musician, etc. For me, this meant playing as many good singer-songwriter gigs as possible, so I could showcase my bass playing (and singing) throughout the local NYC scene.

I began to treat my bass playing much like any business: I ordered business cards, applied for a business license, signed up for a small business checking account at my bank, set up a website and maintained a contact list of musicians that I'd met, noting their phone, email and web information (just like one would do when starting any business). I created a Myspace and Facebook page, and posted ads on CraigsList. Eventually, I was fortunate enough to obtain endorsements from some of my favorite bass companies (Sadowsky Guitars, NYC, Lakland, Euphonic Audio and Rotosound, USA). Live shows, business cards, websites and endorsements are all great ways to advertise yourself for little or no cost.

Although I was always playing bass and studying privately, it wasn't until later that I began the "woodshedding" necessary to keep up with the great players that New York has to offer. When I first moved into the East Village, my wife was working as a public school teacher. For many years I was able to put in eight hour days practicing the bass and learning material. The rest of my day was typically followed by networking via Internet and phone, going out to shows or playing gigs and rehearsals . . .

In addition to playing live shows and recordings, I decided to start teaching bass lessons. I developed my own curriculum tailored to various skill levels and interests, and I created several practice routine options for students contingent upon how much time they had to put in every day. It wasn't long before I had four or five students a day, seven days a week. I attribute my success in attaining so many students directly to free advertising online, taking a lot of work with different bands, and having an up to date performance schedule posted on my website. In fact, in the beginning, very few students found me via word of mouth. Most found me through the Internet and were interested in taking lessons with me because of what they had read on my website.

I offer my services as music director and producer to artists as well. As MD, I act as liaison between management, artist and band to facilitate the demands of a performance, recording or tour. I assist in running rehearsals, hiring musicians and providing any necessary charts for the band. My production services include recommending the appropriate studio(s), hiring musicians (if need be), getting the right engineer on hand, and serving as "producer" inside the studio environment.

To act as yet another medium to get my name out there and to generate more work, I chose to produce two of my own records using some of my favorite musicians. My first record showcased my creative approach to music as well as my improvisational skills, whereas my second CD showcased my singing and songwriting abilities; both of which featured my bass playing. I have since been called to produce and play bass for bands simply because someone took a liking to one of these records or read reviews of them.

When playing bass in the studio for many artists, I paid close attention to the engineer navigating through ProTools and I watched how the producer interacted with the artists. On sessions, I was making connections with various studios, producers and engineers. I made it a goal to learn production skills so that I could offer artists these services.

*   *   *   *   *   *   *   *

If you are the type of person that needs a sense of stability or requires a guaranteed steady income, work as an upcoming bassist in NYC is probably not for you. You are going to have to want it so badly that you are willing to make sacrifices in order to make ends meet: living in an apartment that's substandard compared to what you might be accustomed to, moving away from family and friends, playing bass with bands that might not be the strongest acts, etc. *If you do not feel fulfilled unless you are playing your instrument, than all of these sacrifices will most likely be worth it to you, and NYC just might be the place where you should set up shop.*

It's somewhat ironic that I decided to write and publish this book when the music business is perhaps at its most insecure moment in history. Record labels are shutting down, big recording studios are closing and the economy has plummeted so much so that people are spending less of their dollars on entertainment. Simply put, you will need to be able to do it all in order to survive as a bassist (i.e. live shows, session work, teach lessons, MD, produce . . .). Make sure that your communication skills are up to snuff as well. Take initiative, network and hang! Get the necessary social skills together and be sure to make it obvious that you enjoy what you're doing.

Everybody has a different path to follow, and what has worked for me might not necessarily be the right road for you travel. That's why I have included over thirty interviews with NYC's top bassists for you to read and learn from. By checking out what all of these players have to say, you will be able to make the choices necessary to pursue your goal as a bassist in NYC. Each interview will provide you with a new perspective on what it takes to be a working bassist. Although each player's musical journey is unique and subject to the time in which he/she entered the NYC scene, the content and advice given is timeless, and provides invaluable information to *all* musicians, young and old.

The Interviews

Photo by Tory Williams

Interview with NYC bassist, Johannes Weidenmueller:

Johannes Weidenmueller is one of the most in demand acoustic bass players in New York City and worldwide. Johannes was born in Heidelberg, Germany and, he has been a New York resident since 1991. He has worked with Kenny Werner, Chris Kase, the Hank Jones Trio, Ray Barretto, the Carl Allen-Vincent Herring Quintet, the John Abercrombie Quartet, Ari Hoenig, and the Joe Lovano Trio to name but a few, as well as musicians including Eddie Henderson, Dewey Redman, Randy Brecker, Kenny Wheeler, Toots Thielemans, George Benson, Wynton Marsalis, Joshua Redman, Gary Bartz, Jonny Coles, Clifford Jordan, Joe Chambers and many others.

Johannes makes appearances at many of the major jazz and music festivals around the world and has collaborated in productions with the National Orchestra of Spain, the Balthasar Neumann Orchestra and Choir, Flamenco musician Chano Dominguez and the Indian music ensemble of Gaurav Madzumdar. He has received numerous awards and grants including the Young European Jazz Artist of the Year Award in 1993 and 1996, the Hennessey Jazz Prize 1996 and grants from Arts International and the New School faculty development grant.

As a bass educator, Johannes has been a faculty member of the New School Jazz and Contemporary Music program since 1997. In addition, he is a member of the faculty at the Mannes College of music, and he has taught workshops and clinics at the Banff Center for the Arts, NYU, University of Green Bay, the Amsterdam Conservatory, University of West Virginia, University of N.C. Chapel Hill, Charleston College S.C., Monk Institute Aspen, Middle Tennessee State University, Cal State Bakersfield, University of Central Oklahoma, Jazz Lab in Edmond, OK, CSNM Paris, Arizona state University, Mansfield University PA, Castleton State College Vermont and many others.

(JC) Born in Germany, you have been a New York resident since 1991. What was the NYC jazz scene like when you first arrived and in what ways has it changed?

(JW) I have to say that moving to NYC from Germany was a dream come true for me. I was a little hesitant about it at first, equally intimidated and inspired by the incredibly high level of musicianship and creative energy in the musical community in New York, but decided to take the plunge in the summer of 1991. I enrolled in the jazz program at the New School, which not only got me in contact with many master teachers and players such as Buster Williams, Ron Carter and Dave Holland among others, but also really helped me to connect to a large network of musicians right away. My first ensemble was with Brad Mehldau on piano and Adam Cruz on drums. Chris Potter, Larry Goldings, Sam Yahel and Peter Bernstein were all students at the same time, so you can imagine how inspiring that was. Equally important if not more was playing sessions, mostly at peoples houses, almost every day of the week. 223 Sackett Street in Brooklyn was the place to hang. Drummer Jorge Rossy lived there as well as Kurt Rosenwinkle and Chris Cheek among others. It was a great workshop to experiment, learn tunes, and just play for hours. There were more clubs to hear live jazz in the 90s than there are today. I used go to the Village Gate quite a bit and Bradley's as well. In the beginning, I probably played four to five times a week, mostly little restaurant or café gigs, duos or trios; again, an invaluable experience for learning repertoire and playing with many different musicians. These connections eventually got me my first touring gig, the trio of pianist Hank Jones (and that led to other engagements).

It is difficult to say how the jazz scene has changed, partially because my own vantage point has changed. I make my living touring and I play much less in town, partially because gigs in New York don't pay. I believe musicians still move to New York because they are looking to grow, learn, get their A***S kicked and feed off of the creative energy that is abundant in the music scene. New York is still the place to be in the world if you are a jazz musician. But I also see that the economic realty in New York has made it much harder to survive as an artist. There are far fewer opportunities to play and hear jazz then there were in the 90s. Clubs are closing because they can't afford the exorbitant rents in Manhattan anymore. Rising real estate prices are forcing musicians to move further and further out to the suburbs and take day jobs to support the habit of making music. Going to college in the city will cost you twenty grand a year or more in tuition alone.

In spite of those realities I still recommend the New York experience as invaluable to anyone who is serious about playing jazz, even if it is only for a limited period of time. Playing jazz and improvising is a very interactive craft and can really only be learned through "live" situations with other improvisers, and the New York jazz scene still has an abundance of those.

(JC) If you could select five attributes (musically or personally) that a bassist must have in order to be working here in New York, what would they be?

(JW) Even though the bass has evolved exponentially in the last twenty years, especially as a solo instrument, the fundamentals you need to work on as a bass player hasn't changed that much over time: making everyone in the band and the music as a whole sound really good. This is not only a musical skill, but also most certainly a personality trait. You have to want to make everybody sound good. Most working bass players I know are in one way or another accommodators, facilitators, unifiers; they really enjoy laying the foundation and are not overly concerned with being in the spotlight.

Here are six musical attributes that I believe are essential to being a working bassist on the New York scene:

1. Good time/feel, a good sense of rhythm and groove. The ability to maintain a solid pulse at any tempo without slowing down or speeding up. An awareness of where you place the beat (right in the center, ahead or behind the beat) and a resulting flexibility regarding playing with different feels. An ability to hear and play different subdivisions, groupings, displacements, odd meters, etc.

2. A knowledge of the history of the style of music you are playing.

3. Good sound. Your sound is your signature; it is the first thing that people notice when they listen to you or by which they identify you.

4. Sight reading skills: most of the music I play these days is original music that involves sight-reading.

5. Good listening skills (obviously, although maybe not to everyone). The ear is that by which we communicate.

6. A flexibility and openness towards different musical styles and a willingness to adapt to many different musical situations. As a rule of thumb, the more flexible and versatile you are, the more likely you are called for gigs.

(JC) What is your overall perspective on the jazz community in New York City right now?

(JW) I still view New York as the place to be if you are serious about playing jazz. I feel like I grow and evolve musically and personally every day that I am here even after seventeen years in the city. The community of likeminded musicians is the main reason for that. I can get together with amazing composers/improvisers any time or go out and hear great music any night of the week.

And professionally, most of the connections for the bigger, better paying touring gigs, the ones that actually allow you to make a living playing jazz, go through New York as well. Of course it is also a double edged sword; making a living in New York is not always a picnic. You end up giving up a certain quality of life. That's about priorities and is a choice that every individual has to make for themselves.

(JC) Do you agree that jazz has a more appreciative audience in Europe in comparison to New York? Has it always been this way or is this shift in interest a recent one?

(JW) I think not just jazz, but the arts in general have always been more appreciated in Europe. This is partially because of a much greater emphasis on arts in the educational curriculum where children are taught to recognize the value of the arts early on. The result is an audience that is more appreciative and more knowledgeable about music. The financial aspect of the business is important as well. The arts in most European countries enjoy much bigger government subsidies, which means promoters, clubs, and cultural centers don't have to worry as much about a band being commercially successful. That helps musicians make a more comfortable living playing the music they want to play.

(JC) Can you discuss your "sound?" Who are you currently working with and where can we see you perform?

(JW) Sound is and has to be a very personal affair; it is your voice, the primary and most important expression of your personality, and should therefore be as personal as possible. You should spend a lot of time discovering and developing your sound. I know I have and it is an ongoing process. While equipment and setup play a role in sound, the sound that I get comes primarily from my touch: my fingers, my technique, etc. Because of the difficulties traveling with an upright bass these days, I frequently have to play the "bass du jour" or rented bass. I am able to get my sound pretty much regardless of what the instrument or amplification is (unless the bass is really messed up and unplayable). My concept has always been to try to play with the biggest sound, and the most clarity with the least amount of effort. I think it is also very important to have a concept of what you want to sound like in your "minds ear" and then to try and project that. Of course the instrument, strings, pickup and amplification make a difference. I have a two main upright basses. My touring bass is a 3/4 German flatback, from 1860. It sounds great in many situations and is light, which is why I like to travel with it. My other bass is a French Roundback that records beautifully. It's heavy though so you'll find it mostly on my recordings. I use Thomastic Spirocore Weich strings (the purple ones). They have a little less tension than the red ones and they seem to work well on my basses. For a pickup, I use either the Realist or the Fishman full circle depending on the amp. The house gets a blended signal from my Schertler DynB and my ATM mic. I have an Acoustic Image Clarus and an Epiphany 2x10 that I use for gigs in the city. When I am touring I request the Eden WT 800.

I am working with a lot of different projects: the Kenny Werner Trio, singer Madeleine Peyroux, guitarist Rez Abassi and many more. I am also writing music for a recording with my own band and will start to perform around town in the near future.

www.Bassistis.com
www.JohannesWeidenmueller.com

Bassist: Johannes Weidenmueller
Interviewed by: John Carey

www.JohnCarey.net

Interview with NYC bassist, Jack Daley:

Jack Daley is a bassist, session musician, music director and producer. He has worked with Lenny Kravitz, Joss Stone, Michael Jackson, Janet Jackson, Queen Latifah, Shabba Ranks, Avril Lavigne, Daryl Hall, Alana Davis, Chaka Khan, The Temptations, Natalie Merchant, Iggie Pop, James Brown and Mick Jagger to name a few.

(JC) You have worked with many well known artists. What were some of the stepping stones that led you in the direction towards many of these highly sought after gigs?

(JD) I think like most of us players I started playing at a fairly young age. At ten years old I wanted to play drums although my mother was not that excited about my choice. After leaning up against her Airline record player while listening, or I should say feeling, *25 or 6 to 4* by Chicago, I was hooked. I grew up in Upstate New York and caught the music scene of the 70s. I started playing clubs at sixteen and it was a great time to be playing bass. There were so many great bass players to check out and I think it was really the peak for great session musicians. Also the disco craze was blowing up and it had some ridiculously funky parts to checkout. I played in some of the area's best bands, playing everything from The Who to Chic to *Autumn Leaves* and everything in between. It was a great learning period.

In the 80s when the MTV craze hit, I started a band that captured the vibe of all the new bands riding that wave. Somehow, by default, I ended up being the band's most obvious frontman. So, along with my brother Frank who is a great guitarist, I locked myself in a studio in Saratoga, New York for about three years, developing my studio chops and writing material to get a record deal. Again this was a great learning period, not only technically, but musically, because when you realize as a producer what type of bass playing makes the best sounding record, it is a bit different than the perspective of most bassists. I just think sometimes when you're only dealing with the bass part it's hard to step back and be objective.

I spent three years in that studio and just got up one day thinking, I have to move to New York City now! That same day, a long time friend called me and said his bassist flipped out and he needed someone. I showed up, nailed the audition and got some very encouraging advice from the guitarist in the band, Ronny Drayton (a total badass). He said, "Move here man. You'll get tons of work." I never left.

Ronny was on the money. Within a year I was in thirteen bands playing funk, rock, blues and singer-songwriter gigs. You name it, I did it. My approach was to take any gig that I thought I would sound good doing. It would give me exposure to the most musicians possible, and give me the best chance to be recommended if a good gig came up. It also helped me to pay my rent. This was also when I realized that I was a much better bassist than I would ever be a singer. Besides that, when I play bass I make the worst bass player face. Combine that with me struggling to hit the notes while singing and it just ain't pretty.

(JC) You are known as a bassist that plays many genres of music, but you've often been called for a lot of rock-R&B oriented bass playing.

Is rock-R&B music what you enjoy playing the most or is it simply the work that found you, so to speak?

(JD) Well as I said before, when growing up in the 70s, it was songs like *Skin Tight*, by the Ohio Players, *For the Love of Money*, by the O'Jays, *Lowdown*, by Boz Scaggs and anything by Chic that really caught my ear first. I believe that's where my interpretation of groove comes from. It was a bit later that I really started checking out more rock players guys like John Entwistle, Paul McCartney and of course John Paul Jones. So yeah, I think rock and funk are really the two genres that I have spent most of my time playing, so it makes sense. That is also why I was so well suited for the Lenny Kravitz gig. Most people think of that as a rock gig which it is, but Lenny feels everything from the perspective of a funk musician and that is really the heart of his music.

(JC) I heard that your 1966 Fender Jazz bass is your axe of choice. Is this true and if so, what attributes does the bass have that attracts you to it? Are there any other basses that you just can't do without?

(JD) You know I love them all; basses are just so cool. My longtime companion is my black 1966 Fender Jazz bass. I don't know what it is but I've never played a bad 1966 Jazz bass, crazy! I have a great 1965 candy apple red Fender Precision bass that I have used on many records. It's also killer. I have a great 1973 Rickenbacker that I love, and I just received a bass from a new company called Henman Bevilaqua. It's very cool and combines a vintage vibe with some very cutting edge technology. I'm really enjoying getting to know this one. The other instrument that I'm thrilled with is my black Hofner Club. It was the very first black Hofner made custom for me. I've got a thing for black.

(JC) I first discovered you when listening to an Alana Davis CD (*Blame It on Me*). Can you discuss what it was like working with her?

(JD) Playing with Alana was always a true joy. I worked on all three of her records and loved every minute of it. I just don't understand why she is not a huge star. She really is a great talent. Some of my favorite bass lines on her records were really very spontaneous. The way she sings really connects for me, and we would sometimes demo her songs at the producer, Ed Tuten's, loft. Ed is a great producer and he's not afraid to keep a first take. Alana's voice is so inspiring to me and her pocket is so deep that it feels like my bass is playing itself. Many of those bass tracks were literally first takes that made the record. I should also mention the drummer on those records . . . Nir Z is one of my favorites to track with.

(JC) What "business" advice can you give to those who are already competent bass players working in NYC, but are seeking work with higher profile bands and artists?

(JD) Well I know it's not easy, but referring to something I said before: get out there and play with everyone that you can shine with. When the Lenny gig came up, I came home to about fifteen calls on my machine (pre cell phone). That is because I had made a lot of friends playing around the city. Also show up on time, be prepared, and try not to lose your cool (I'm actually reminding myself on that one). Also, and this is very important, have fun! If music is not gonna be fun you might as well work for the man. At least there you'll get health insurance.

www.MySpace.com/JackPDaley

Bassist: Jack Daley
Interviewed by: John Carey

www.JohnCarey.net

Interview with NYC bassist, Patrick Pfeiffer:

Patrick Pfeiffer is a bass player and teacher, author of *Bass Guitar for Dummies* and *Improve Your Groove, The Ultimate Guide for Bass*, as well as the book, *In Search of the Daily Groove*. He is the leader of his own band, Phoenix. Patrick was born in Bremen, Germany, and later studied Jazz Performance at Arizona State University followed by earning a masters degree in Jazz at New England Conservatory in Boston. In Massachusetts, Patrick worked with George Russell, Jimmy Guiffre, Mick Goodrick and Sheila Jordan. After graduation, he moved to New York and worked with George Clinton, Jimmy Norman (of The Coasters), Bernard Purdie, Mikki Howard, Carlos Alomar, Lady Kyra, Phoebe Snow, Gary Corwin and the Dream Band to name a few.

(JC) You teach everyone from beginners to professionals. What do you find yourself teaching most to those students interested in maintaining bass work here in New York City?

(PF) Whatever their challenges may be, I help players on all levels to get past them. It's different for each individual, but there are some things that come up again and again. Often I teach the road-warriors and hard-bitten veterans ways to build up and maintain their endurance. A special set of specific right and left hand etudes usually does the trick. I also take care of any problems they may have with their technique. Essentially, I make it easier for them to do their "thing." They also get a short warm-up to do before each gig that helps them get into their "zone."

Sometimes players who are usually hired for one specific style would like to branch out, but need a hand getting past the thing they are known for, so I cover different genres and styles with them, and all the bells and whistles that come with the new territory. A rock player will certainly be excellent at playing on the beat, but may need to work on the sixteenth note off-beats for some serious funk playing. It opens up opportunities for them to branch out and play with other artists, or get ready for the next gig once their gig dries up.

As far as the smoking players who are still under the radar screen, it's basically the same idea: teaching them about warming up, endurance, versatility, technique, speed, rhythm and harmony, and how to create a groove or a solo. But I also teach them about taking care of their needs first. A lot of bass players have day jobs here in New York City; it's simply way too expensive to survive while you're waiting for that next gig. I help them devise a warm up that they can do at the start of the day, before they do anything else, like going to work. This helps them keep things in perspective and honor their "inner bassist" first before anything else can get in the way. In my early days in New York I developed a routine for myself that I did each morning, and I felt like a bass player for the rest of the day, even though I was fixing health-food sandwiches for people. Besides, it enabled me to be in top form when that call finally did come.

As far as the raw beginners are concerned, I get them started on the right foot, both technically as well as musically. They have the advantage of not having any bad habits yet, so if I give them the proper exercises and expose them to some great music from the start, then it won't be long before they join the rank of the players.

(JC) What tips do you give your students to find and maintain work as bassists here in NYC?

(PF) I tell my students to always be ready to play; that means being warmed up for the day. That's first and foremost, because they get only one chance to make a first impression. If they're warmed up, then at the very least they'll play well. The next item on the agenda is versatility. New York is such a colorful and multi-cultural place, a bass player really needs to be versatile in as many different genres and styles as possible. Going from a funk gig to a Latin gig and getting an offer to do a Top 40 gig that weekend is not all that unusual.

I also tell them to be impeccable with their word. If they agree to a gig, make sure they're there on time, prepared, playing their absolute best, and doing it with a smile and a great attitude. Personality is very important to any musician. Make it fun to be around you, and make good music in the process. This will lead to people asking you for your phone number. It really helps the networking process when you're a nice cat.

At the NYC Bass Brunch, Will Lee told everyone that every gig he did, no matter how large or small, he'd go, "Yeah, man! This is the shit! This is it! This is great!" I found that so inspiring to hear from a heavy hitter like him to still get so excited about everything he does. No wonder people love hiring him. Of course, it helps that he plays so well and tastefully.

(JC) As a bass instructor, can you talk about some of the pleasures you have had teaching people over the years? What opportunities have you been given as a direct result from teaching electric bass?

(PF) One of the greatest pleasures I get is to have to transcribe one of my student's bass lines. Sometimes someone will take one of my teachings and put a new spin on it, and it's just great, because I may never have thought of it in that way. I constantly learn from my students, both from their successes as well as their questions.

Another big pleasure I get is seeing all those light bulb moments when we do the bass and drum seminars, and they see that the stuff I teach them really does work in a playing situation. The biggest pleasure of all is knowing that I've had a hand in creating some awesome bass players who will contribute mightily to the bass community.

(JC) What basses and amplifiers are you using?

(PF) My basses are three awesome MTD six-strings, one fretted, two fretless. Michael Tobias, the luthier (MTD stands for "Michael Tobias Design"), is my hero. He really knows how to put his passion for building basses into his instruments, so they can fuel our passion for playing bass. All three basses have a very powerful and focused tone, amazing playability, and great dynamic range. I couldn't ask for more from an instrument.

The amp I use is a Walter Woods ultra. Man, it's beautiful. I have two of them so that I don't have to worry about playing through anything else if one goes into "the shop" (that's Walter Wood's shop), which may happen maybe once a decade. The Walter Woods is very powerful, clean, clear and portable. It makes the instruments sound at their best, so the better the instrument, the better the sound out of the amp. I also just got a very cool little amp, a Mark Bass II, which was a very generous gift from a friend. I love that one as well, and for the same reasons.

I just switched to Epifani cabinets, the 3x10 and the 2x10 ultralight series. They're excellent! Clean and clear, plenty of punch, which I love, and a very focused bass sound. They too, are very portable, not for their size, but for their weight. Right now I feel like my gear is state of the art.

(JC) Can you discuss what it was like for you as a player when you first moved to New York City and how has the scene changed since you arrived?

(PF) When I first came to the City, there was still ample opportunity to play at jam sessions. The Village was filled with little and big clubs that had weekly jams going, usually jazz, blues or rock. I really got to hone my skills in a live situation that way, and even hosted a few jams. We also had more opportunities to hear great musicians live at very reasonable prices.

It's a little different now, less jam sessions around town, although I feel it's coming back again. There are fewer opportunities for inexperienced players to jam in front of an audience; it's mostly reserved for the veterans now. The jams have become much more selective in who gets to sit in, which is too bad, because how else is a young cat going to learn what it's like to play music in a live situation?

One thing that has improved in my opinion is the infamous "New York attitude," that cutthroat competitive behavior. It seems that 9/11 has exposed people's true colors, and they're beautiful. I see older bass players helping out younger ones to get their playing together, connect with the right players, constructively critique their playing and help them network. It seems like the players have gotten a softer attitude, which helps everyone. I think we're moving in the right direction and I'm glad to be part of it.

www.sourkrautmusic.com

Bassist: Patrick Pfeiffer
Interviewed by: John Carey

www.JohnCarey.net

Interview with NYC bassist, Neil Jason:

Neil Jason is a professional bassist, producer and composer born and raised in New York City. He has worked with John Lennon, Yoko Ono, Billy Joel, Roxy Music, Bryan Ferry, Hall & Oats, Mick Jagger, Pete Townshend, Charlie Watts, Carly Simon, Paul Simon, Kiss, Janis Ian, Harry Chapin, Debbie Harry, Joe Jackson, Michael Jackson, Diana Ross, Gladys Night, The Brecker Brothers, Bob James, David Sanborn, Celine Dion, John McLaughlin, Michael Franks, Cindy Lauper, Dire Straits, Eddie Van Halen and Pavorotti to name a few. In addition, he was a member of the house band for *Saturday Night Live* from 1983 to 1985. Neil has also worked on countless hit commercials throughout the years of being a bassist here in NYC.

(JC) In what ways has the NYC music scene changed over the years with regard to getting work as a bassist, from both the studio and live perspective?

(NJ) It changes, and yet it cycles around and starts again. I chose to stay in NYC in the beginning of my career because there were so many places to play live. All different types of clubs, all kinds of bands needed. That seemed to change for a while, clubs disappeared, venues changed. But now, I see an incredible resurgence of live playing, great new clubs and more tours. The only way to get the work is to get out there. Audition everywhere, for anything. Almost any live gig is worth it if you need the experience, and you need to be seen.

Now the studio world . . . well that's a different scene. The recording studio and the recording process have been reinvented enough to make it readily available to almost anyone. What used to be a very centralized (big studio) and very expensive (tons of gear), is now inexpensive and portable. The studio work you get will come through your live gigs and contacts initially. Take advantage of the technology. Learn a program. Watch a great engineer. Get the knowledge that will help you sound better, quicker, the next time you record.

(JC) If you had to choose five attributes (musically or personally) that a bassist must have in order to survive as a working bassist here in NYC, what would they be?

(NJ) Great question. Let's start with the simple one that's not so simple.

1. Be on time. Sounds easy, huh? I knew a lot of cats who just could not be on time, and these guys were good. But eventually someone more dependable gets the call. Show respect for the artist, the music and yourself. Be on time.

2. Be prepared. Is my gear in top shape? Do I have extra everything? Carry tools and know how to use em.

3. Be open to new musical experiences. You never know what might come up stylistically on a session. Be a student and a pro. Learn to listen and practice what surprises you so you're ready the next time.

4. Stay in shape. Touring, gigging and constant session work can wear you down physically and mentally. Pay attention to your health. It will help you play better, longer.

5. HAVE FUN!!! Smile, you're playing bass and doing what you love. It doesn't get any better than this.

(JC) What advice can you give to those bassists who are already competent bass players in NYC, but are seeking work with higher profile artists?

(NJ) Again, the more you play, the more people you meet and the more opportunities you will have. Just be ready. You never know which gig or demo might lead to a step up.

(JC) How do you approach tracking a bass line for pop, rock or R&B artists? In your opinion, what makes a good bass line in this setting?

(NJ) Ah yes . . . coming up with a bassline. You need to pay attention to the song, the style, the artist, the producer and the drummer. Marry the drummer if you have to, but you need to be "one" with him to make a track work. You need to do it so many times that you learn to internalize this input and go right to the FEEL. You're in the rhythm section. You need to support the changes and the groove. Different drummers lay the groove in different spots. Learn to adjust. Listen to your tone. Make it work for you. More low end? Less low end? Longer notes? Fingers? Pick? Fretless? And make sure you're comfortable with your part. If you need to run it under headphones while everyone eats lunch, do it. The only thing that matters is the good take. If it's live, you wanna be ready for the magic. If it's an overdub, you wanna know your part so you can be creative and not waste time. Write your own charts or cheat sheet if needed. Anything you need to free yourself up to be more creative.

(JC) How would you describe your "feel" and "sound," and what basses are you currently using?

(NJ) I think my feel lies in my ability to read drummers grooves and my own internal time clock. Sometimes I feel I can see all the tiny subdivisions between the beats and I just pick the spot that feels tight with the drums. Remember, I was blessed with some of the finest drummers in the world to play with. When you play with the "A Team," it elevates your game. I used to play along with my favorite bass lines on records to learn the feel. The more you do it, the more you develop your own groove. Sound is a whole different animal. It all starts with your bass. Your touch on that axe is the start of your sound. In the studio you need to work with the engineer and listen to playbacks to make adjustments. Live, you need to trust your gear and the engineer. Soundcheck is important; on stage there is no "Take 2."

My main bass has been a stock 63 L series Fender Jazz bass. I've used it on hundreds of albums and it still sounds amazing. My other favorite bass is a Sadowsky fretless that Roger made for me when he first started and I use it often. There's always a specialty bass that I might need for a song, but I found that with a jazz, a precision, and a fretless, a little foam, and some cool EQ, you could pretty much find any sound you want.

www.MySpace.com/NeilJason

Bassist: Neil Jason
Interviewed by: John Carey

www.JohnCarey.net

Interview with NYC bassist, Tim Lefebvre:

Tim Lefebvre is a professional bassist in New York City. Tim has made appearances in *Saturday Night Live's* house band over the last several years. His work can also be heard on *The Departed, The Apprentice, The Sopranos, Late Show With David Letterman, The Knights of Prosperity* (CBS), *30 Rock* (NBC), *Oceans 12, Ocean's 13, KT Tunstall, Harold & Kumar Go To White Castle*, and *Analyze That!*. He has made appearances with Jamie Cullum, Chris Botti, Mario Cantone, Chris Potter's Underground, Rudder, Uri Caine Bedrock, Jon Bon Jovi, James Taylor, Josh Groban, Nellie McKay, JJ Appleton, Emily Zuzik, Oz Noy, Wayne Krantz and Melissa Errico. He also produces his very own ringtones!

(JC) How long have you been involved with the New York City music scene and what was it like when you first arrived?

(TL) I moved to NYC in 1993. I was so excited to be here. The city had a different energy then . . . much more chaotic and refreshing. I wanted to play with so many cats. And there were lots of great guys then for me to look up to. My heroes from the 80s were still on the scene . . . Omar Hakim, Darryl Jones, Tain Watts, Reggie Washington, Wayne Krantz, Victor Bailey, Kenny Kirkland, Kenny Garrett and many more. The scene then was different than it is now. I think the jingle scene was just petering out, as well as the session scene. Now things on that front are less formal (i.e. less union involvement and at smaller studios) and scarcer (anyone can program bass and drums for a commercial nowadays . . . and strings for that matter). Guys who used to make good livings on that kind of work are doing other kinds of gigs now.

(JC) Can you discuss the importance of playing all genres of music? What artists and bands have you worked with that have required the knowledge of multiple genres?

(TL) I think it's really important if you want to make a good living at this. I am blessed with the opportunity to play acoustic bass with Patti Austin, then turn around and thrash out with Rudder, JJ Appleton or Emily Zuzik on electric. Or sub for James Genus on *SNL* (which is an intense mix of reading charts and playing with an old school R&B feel/aesthetic), then record a record on acoustic with MOSS or Peter Eldridge.

(JC) What is your take on the importance of reading music well here in New York? Also, do you believe that a formal music education is necessary in order to be a working bassist?

(TL) I think it's moderately important to be a good reader. It comes back to the versatility question: how many genres do you want to be able to play well? If the answer for you is many, then you better be a kick ass reader. There are projects (especially with the young whippersnappers) where the artist writes *hard*-ass music, so you have to be ready to deal with that. Wayne Krantz's music was like that. But Wayne was patient enough to let me get what he wrote into my ear, which helped my reading immensely.

On the other hand, there are also lots of projects on the pop end of things where reading is not incredibly necessary . . . maybe an understanding of chord charts is more apropos. So it's a tossup.

I myself am not formally educated in music. I got my BA in Economics and Political Science from the University of Rochester. Some of the smartest people I know (Zach Danziger being one of them) never went to college at all, and are successful in the music biz. So I don't think it's a requirement to have gone to college at all.

(JC) What are your main basses and amps these days?

(TL) I am back to using my 65 Jazz on a lot of stuff. It's just a magic axe. . . warm and funky. Also I have been playing my Matthias Thoma upright I bought from my friend Ruben at Brooklyn Brass and Reed. It's a decent sounding carved bass that is pretty easy to play. It also records pretty well . . . it's got that bright carved sound. I used it on the soundtrack to *The Departed*. The tradeoff of huge sound vs. playability has been something I have been experimenting with over the last couple of years.

I also have been using my 77 P bass a lot, especially when I travel. It's not as versatile as my Jazz but it sounds pretty killer, and I am not so in love with it that if the airline made me check it and broke it, I would not be completely heartbroken. And I love that 80s roundwound picked sound, a la Adam Clayton and Peter Hook. Whenever needed, I also use my Epiphone Allen Woody semi hollow body. Pretty wicked with a Sansamp!

Amp-wise, an SVT full-on rig would be perfect, but short of that I like Eden 4X10 cabs with SWR heads.

(JC) Recently you have been working a lot with The Oz Noy Trio. Can you talk about your overall experience playing with Oz? And what made you decide to pull out the trusty old Fender Precision bass?

(TL) Oz's gig is fun. It's loosely based on familiar sounding grooves, but with a twist thrown in. He is also a gifted guitarist, and very adept with effects. And I have had the pleasure of doing the gig with some of my favorite drummers . . . Anton Fig, Rocky Bryant, Tony Escapa and Keith Carlock. They all give the music a unique slant, so that makes it really fun.

In terms of the P bass, I had just been hearing that sound for a long time. In fact I was not using the back pickup in my jazz basses in an attempt to get the P bass sound. I rarely use anything else but my Fenders, but when I need or I'm hearing five string I bust out my Sadowsky five. It's a great sounding axe.

www.MySpace.com/SkipHerbertson

Bassist: Tim Lefebvre
Interviewed by: John Carey

www.JohnCarey.net

Interview with NYC bassist, Conrad Korsch:

Conrad Korsch is a professional acoustic and electric bassist in New York City. Born and raised in Philadelphia, he earned a B.A. in Jazz Bass Performance from Temple University. Conrad has worked with Rod Stewart, Carly Simon, Roseanne Cash, Joan Osborne, Madeleine Peyroux, Carole King, Marc Cohn, Andrea Bocelli, Bette Midler, Gavin DeGraw, Clay Aiken and Deborah Gibson, in addition to working in the Broadway show, *Swing!*. He has also been a substitute for the *Saturday Night Live* house band and several Broadway shows. Conrad is a singer-songwriter himself, and is currently recording his original material and performing solo shows in between (and during) world tours with Rod Stewart. He has taught for the University of the Arts, Swarthmore College, NYC Bass Collective, Sam Ash Music Institute (Manhattan), NARAS "Grammy in the Schools" program and is a member of Local 802 of the American Federation of Musicians.

(JC) At what age did you enter the New York City music scene, and what were your initial impressions?

(CK) When I was twenty-two, I graduated Temple University with a Bachelor's Degree in Jazz Bass Performance and moved to NYC two months later. I started sitting in at jam sessions at jazz clubs all over the city: the jam at the Bitter End on Sunday nights, playing in a community orchestra, and taking lessons . . . trying to check out as many scenes as I could. The thing that really struck me the most was the need to know tunes, particularly in the jazz sessions. Nothing was off limits. When I was in school I used to carry four different "Real Books" to gigs and it was okay to read. I played Saturday nights with Jimmy Bruno in Philly the last couple years I was in school. He used to just start playing and make me follow him without giving me time to find tunes in the books, so I'd learn a lot of tunes that way. After moving to New York I realized that nobody was pulling out books and there were hundreds of more tunes that I needed to know so I made a point of memorizing at least a half dozen a week. I did the same with funk and R&B tunes . . . particularly ones where the bass line carried the song, so that I wouldn't get stuck trying to fake my way through *Brickhouse*, for example.

(JC) How have you seen the state of the music business change since you moved here, specifically with regard to getting work as a sideman?

(CK) Unfortunately (or fortunately, depending how you look at it), I missed the big glorious studio days that led up into the 80s (five jingles a day, a record date, then a club gig when not on tour = house in the Hamptons, driver to take you to/from sessions, cartage company, etc.). So I don't have the same observations or complaints that a lot of my older friends have. Since I've been here, I've noticed a lot more heavy musicians embracing the stability and convenience of a Broadway gig. I've also been on wedding gigs with people whose music I studied in school, so I think there's generally more of an appreciation for live "work" now, particularly since so many recording jobs have been lost to virtual instruments and the ability of producer/engineers to ProTools edit marginal playing into something acceptable. New clubs continue to pop up, and the singer-songwriter scene on the lower east side is thriving, but the loss of such scenes as Tuesday nights at the Metropolitan has definitely left a gap in the NYC music scene for a certain type of playing and hang.

(JC) What advice can you give to those bassists here in New York who are looking for work with higher profile artists?

(CK) The way that I ended up playing with most of these people was through connections that I'd made on much smaller gigs in clubs, restaurants, etc. I first met drummer Shawn Pelton when we both took a seventy-five dollar gig in a restaurant playing jazz and blues with pianist Paul Tillotson. Shawn is an example of a musician who doesn't need to schlep his gear around to clubs to make small change, but still does it because it gives him an opportunity to musically stretch out in a different way and to continue to meet new people and stay connected to the live music scene in the city. Since that gig, I've done a ton of different things with Shawn, and because of our musical connection he has brought me in on some of the most high profile gigs I've done, e.g.: *Saturday Night Live* house band and Rod Stewart. When I first moved to town I took every gig I could get just so people would hear me play and I'd meet people. You never know who you're going to end up on the bandstand with. When I'm in between tours I take singer-songwriter gigs, jazz gigs, recording sessions, sub on Broadway, even some weddings and other corporate gigs just to flex the musical muscles that I don't use with Rod and to meet new people. It's still common for me to meet for the first time a great musician who's lived in NYC for longer than I have, but whose path I've never crossed. That's the way it's worked for me. Some people get wind of auditions, but I've hardly been in that loop. I've only done a handful of auditions in fourteen years, and often when they have a big "cattle call" audition for something, they still end up giving the gig to somebody that the musical director knew from some other gig . . .

(JC) What five attributes (musically or personally) must a bassist have, in your opinion, in order to get and maintain work here in NYC?

(CK)
1. No less than six strings on your bass.
2. The ability to tap.

3. Amplifier with minimum 2000 watts and solid state electronics a must... tubes just sound so "old."
4. Always be overconfident and tell people you are "the man" at whatever they ask, even if you have no experience in that particular field.
5. Make sure that when you meet someone you verbally give them your entire resume in the first two minutes of conversation, and then ask them what their name is again while looking around the room and never making direct eye contact...

OK, seriously, it depends on what kind of work you want to do, but generally:

1. I am a big proponent of reading. The ability to sight-read music will open up the doors to many other work opportunities versus not being able to read.
2. Be as versatile as you can and learn (memorize) the important repertoire of the styles you choose.
3. Maintain your gear.
4. Be prepared, on time, fun, friendly and put your ego aside so that you can play what's appropriate for the music.
5. Apply the opposite of the first five things I said above...

(JC) What are your main basses for studio and live work?

(CK) For a session, I usually ask what kind of track it is, what kind of sound they are looking for (bright, thumpy, modern, retro), and if they need a five string for the extra low notes. If nothing is specified I always just grab my '72 Fender Jazz bass with by-passable Sadowsky preamp installed since it's versatile and always sounds great just plugged straight in. I have hipshot D-tuners on all of my four string basses except for my Danelectro, so I can usually get away with playing a four string on most things unless they want me to ride a low C or something. I have flatwounds on my Danelectro; when I'm in town, I often bring it to my weekly Birdland/Tommy Igoe Big Band gig since it has a kind of thumpy thing to it. It's not as limiting as the upright when we do Jaco or Michel

Camilo charts. I also love my '66 Fender Precision. On tour with Rod, I'm currently using an Alleva-Coppolo four string and a Lakland five string Joe Osborne model. I leave my "Conrad Copper" Alleva-Coppolo five string and my Lakland four string at home for NYC work. My main upright is a Juzek, and I have a plywood Kay that I used in the Broadway show *Swing!* and currently leave out on tour with Rod Stewart for when we do the *American Songbook* stuff. I use David Gage "Realist" pickups and PIRASTRO gut or synthetic gut strings wrapped in metal on both of them. I also have an Azola "Lightning Bug" electric upright bass that I use with MOJO MANCINI because I can crank it up and run it through effects with no feedback. I've also used that bass with Manhattan Transfer and others as a travel-friendly acoustic bass alternative and it's always sounded great. I have a Rob Allen fretless five string with nylon tape wound strings that sounds and looks beautiful and unique. DR High Beams are on all of my other electric basses.

www.ConradKorsch.com
www.MySpace.com/ConradKorsch

Bassist: Conrad Korsch
Interviewed by: John Carey

www.JohnCarey.net

Interview with NYC bassist & producer, Mark Plati:

Mark Plati is a bassist, producer and mixer in New York City. His past and present clients include David Bowie, The Cure, Shawn Colvin, Prince, Brazilian Girls, Natalie Imbruglia, Earl Slick, IVY, Heather Eatman, Anik Jean, Louise Attaque, Eden Ants, Dave Navarro, Les Rita Mitsouko, Hooverphonic, Michael Stipe, Alisha's Attic, Junior Vasquez, Arthur Baker, Alain Bashung, New Order, Suzanne Vega, Marc Cohn, Ruth Ruth, Duncan Sheik, Robbie Williams, Riuichi Sakamoto and Quincy Jones, among many others.

(JC) How long have you been working in New York City as a bassist and as a producer? How would you describe the music scene when you first began working here, with regard to getting work as a bassist and producer?

(MP) I arrived bright and early in January of 1987 fresh off an internship in Dallas, Texas, where I'd worked on a 48-track remote recording truck for no pay, and supported myself as a bassist in bar bands. That makes it, oh, twenty-one years now. At that time there were tons of studios in New York, so there were a lot of doors to knock on. Bass players were certainly working . . . I was lucky enough to record Anthony Jackson, Chuck Rainey, Verdine White and Doug Wimbish, as well as sneak on a few recordings myself. But in 1987 MIDI was king, so my basses didn't see a whole lot of action the first years I was making my way up the engineer/mixing ladder. People sure loved the control of sequencing the bass, and that sound was in vogue for fifteen minutes or so. Lucky for all of us, that phase is long gone.

(JC) How has the scene changed from a bassist's perspective, as well as from the standpoint of a producer?

(MP) I'm not sure I'm the one to ask. I've had my own little niche for quite some time now, and getting a good, general read on the state of the industry can be tricky. Though that's also a very telling thing . . . how music production has become more and more "niche." So many people are doing what I'm doing . . . working out of their own room, with their own rig, and sending/receiving files over the Internet, and phoning it in, so to speak . . . this year especially. So far, over 75% of my work has been unattended mixing or performance.

I've seen the dynamic change from what I'd describe as the classic NYC recording scene . . . one of a myriad of studios, players and services, and all the indulgences you could throw in . . . to today, where we've got a few high end rooms, a few specialty studios, and then a bunch of guys like myself with above-average to top-notch workspaces. The combination of the shrinking of recording budgets, as well as the availability of recording technology (as well as knowledge) has changed the landscape. I certainly couldn't have had a room as capable as mine ten years ago, nor would I have bothered to; the necessity for it simply wasn't there. Gone are the days of taking five hours to get a snare sound, or having a studio charge you $100 for a plate of croissants. For many, it's a good thing.

Still, in the bass world I'd think it's better than ever in some ways. There is always a demand for good musicianship, and those who can turn up and do the job quickly and capably will always be in demand. Getting paid fairly and timely seems to be more challenging, especially over the past six months . . . people have been complaining to me a lot!

(JC) Considering the current state of the music business, what would you recommend to those bassists in NYC who are already competent bassists, but are seeking work with higher profile artists?

(MP) Nothing . . . not management, an attorney, or a label deal works like good ol' word of mouth (or maybe a good YouTube clip). So, be good at what you do, live it and breathe it and eat it for breakfast, and eventually you will become known for it. Make the pursuit of quality your mission. Seek out others, and situations where you'll be visible in a way that showcases what you're about. Once you're a known quantity, you'll get filed in people's mental Rolodex (yikes, dating myself), and you'll occupy a good spot in the musical gene pool. Then it's all up to chance to some extent. I didn't court any of the artists you mentioned. Either I was sought out or already working with somebody they happened to be in contact with. It's the same old story: be patient for the opportunity, but be more than ready when it comes.

(JC) As a producer, who are some of your favorite bassists to have in the studio?

(MP) Well, recording Anthony Jackson was fabulous. You hear stories about people, and I'd heard he was demanding and difficult. I found him to be a real gentleman, and simply genuinely concerned that his performance be the best it could possibly be. Sure, he was demanding. Anybody striving for excellence rightly tends to be.

I've recorded Gail Ann Dorsey loads of times. She is so underrated, simply because her voice is so awesome that people tend to focus on it. I was lucky enough to track Wayne Pedzwater; he was sight-reading on a gig . . . that sure made me go home and bone up on the black dots (as well as tackle a few more hills on my bike).

(JC) What attributes do you feel that a studio bassist must have (musically or personally) in order to be a top notch session player in the pop, rock and R&B genres?

(MP) You've got to embrace all kinds of music and know what they're about from the ground up. You've got to know your history, where these patterns and grooves and feels came from, and which well to draw from when the situation dictates. Never, ever stop being a student; never stop learning. Having a margarita with the artist or discussing last night's Yankee game with the assistant doesn't hurt either.

www.MySpace.com/MarkPlati
www.Mark-Plati.com

Bassist & Producer: Mark Plati
Interviewed by: John Carey

www.JohnCarey.net

Photo by John Carey

Interview with NYC bassist, Steve Jenkins:

Steve Jenkins is a bassist, solo artist and instructor in New York City. He began playing electric bass at age thirteen. Steve has worked with David "Fuze" Fiuczynski, Adam Deitch, Jeff Bhasker, Sam Kininger, Charles Haynes, Vernon Reid, Ingrid Michaelson, Thomas Pridgen (The Mars Volta), Wayne Krantz, Corey Glover, Screaming Headless Torsos, Dean Bowman, DJ Logic, Stephanie McKay (Astralwerks recording artist), Adam Deitch, Steve Hunt, Eric Krasno (Soulive), Hiromi (telarc jazz recording artist), Jeff "Skunk" Baxter, John Blackwell (drummer for Prince), Sean Rickman, Federico Gonzalez Pena and many others. Steve is currently a member of Screaming Headless Torsos, David Fiuczynski's KIF and Vernon Reid's solo project, Masque.

(JC) When did you move to New York City and what were your initial impressions when you first entered the scene?

(SJ) I moved to NYC at the end of 2004. I already knew lots of people in NYC so it wasn't that hard to adjust. Also, I had been coming down fairly regularly to see people play or do gigs. I already knew what the deal was and what to expect. I guess my impression of NYC is based on what I've heard from the people who have been in it for decades and people who are newer to the city like me. I have been here almost four years. I guess on good days I like it and on bad days I want to leave and never come back. That is just part of how it goes here. Having said that, the worst day in the life of a professional musician is probably better than a good day at most other jobs.

(JC) Monetarily speaking, what can you recommend to players new to NYC so that they can make rent and remain here in New York as a working bassist?

(SJ) Teaching lessons has worked for me as far as that goes but it does take some time to find students and maintain a decent roster. I would probably say initially to that person trying to stick around and make their rent: find a day gig. There are tons of day gigs that won't interfere with what happens at night time in terms of playing work. I don't care what people say. That "starving artist" lifestyle is complete bullshit. It is hard to stay creative and positive when money isn't coming in. At least for me it is. It's good and necessary to lock down some income to a certain degree. Just make sure you don't become so comfortable that you settle into your day gig and phase the "real" reason for being here out (which would be the music and finding playing work).

(JC) What do you see yourself doing twenty-five years from now? Would you like to remain in NYC? What do you think your main focus might be musically?

(SJ) I'm not really sure what I'm going to be doing in twenty-five years from now (let alone twenty-five days from now). I know that wanting to make music will be the motivating factor in my life. I have a natural tendency to want to evolve and stretch the boundaries of what I know. The rest I couldn't tell you. The music business and the economy are both so bad at this point. Who knows what will happen? If NYC continues the way it is going over the next decade (higher and higher rents, clubs closing, disappearing culture, etc.), I could see leaving after a certain point. But for now, I love it and could not imagine being anywhere else.

(JC) What steps are you taking (if any) to provide yourself with financial security?

(SJ) First, I have an IRA which I put money in regularly. It's a smart idea and they are not hard to set up.

Also, not that it means that much in terms of getting gigs, but I *do* have my degree from Berklee College of Music which would look good on a resume.

And lastly, having a diverse set of skills that maybe extends beyond just being a bass player will help. For example, right now I am developing my production skills, and I am hoping to make a career shift at some point. I like the idea of making and selling tracks for TV spots and multimedia purposes. It is not something that I have had a lot of experience with thus far, but I make tracks for fun all the time and I have begun to assemble a demo reel. The idea of working on a thirty second piece of music and making some money from that is far more appealing to me than a four hour club date where I would have to play crap like *Dancing Queen* or *Celebration*. I certainly don't feel bad about admitting that either.

Also, I think that being only a sideman puts you at a disadvantage business-wise because you are at the mercy of whoever you work for. If the artists you play for decide they don't want to play or tour, you are out of work. Simple as that. And unless they put you on retainer, that means no money at all. So, the other thing I suggest is become a leader and put together your own projects. That way you can make sure no matter what, you have something to do.

(JC) How would you describe the bass community in New York City?

(SJ) On the surface, everyone seems to be cool, supportive and friendly, but it *is* competitive. And I'm not dissing anyone specifically but I do think it tends to get downplayed in many interviews that I read about the NYC scene.

Having said all of that, I have some great friends here who happen to be awesome bass players. And besides being inspiring musicians, they have helped me out considerably ever since I moved here. That, more than anything, should be very telling about how the bass community ultimately is here.

(JC) If you had to choose only five attributes a bass player must have in order to be a working bassist here in New York, what would they be?

(SJ) This is a tough question because there are so many different kinds of gigs and they don't always call for the same kinds of skills. But here are five general things that I think all bass players need to have to work anywhere: a good groove, playing with conviction, good ears, creativity, and knowing yourself musically. If I could tack on a bonus one: No matter what, always be cool. I once heard Meshell Ndegéocello say that the bass player is the coolest motherfucker in the band. It's part of the role we play. I think she's right.

www.SteveJenkinsBass.com

**Bassist: Steve Jenkins
Interviewed by: John Carey**

www.JohnCarey.net

Interview with L.I./NYC bassist, Jerry McDonald:

Jerry McDonald is an upright and electric bass player working in the Long Island and the NY Metro area. He has worked with Tim Siciliano, Paul Micca, The Swingset Quartet with Jennifer Morgo, Steve Salerno, John Macurrio, Soul Revival, Ben Bynum, Kenny Mackenzie, Matt Wynne, Shenole Latimer, Jack's Waterfall, Frank Bellucci, Skipp Scott, Mark Marino, Cindy Lopez, Bobby Sexton, Leslie Mendelson and many more . . . Jerry has toured Russia with the Anastasia Renee Quartet and he is currently the bassist for the Al Miller Big Band.

(JC) You are one of the few professional upright players to have only begun studying the instrument since the age of thirty. Can you explain how playing the electric bass at a younger age eventually led you to being primarily an upright player? And how did learning cello in high school play a part?

(JM) I actually started playing electric bass in college; I probably was almost twenty years old at that time. As can be typical, my friends were starting a band and needed a bass player so I decided to fill the chair. I was always passionate about music and thought of taking up the electric bass before this situation arose. I never thought at the time that I would become a professional bass player. I studied business in college and worked in corporate America for a few years, but I always continued to play on the side in different bands. In my late twenties after playing a lot of rock and blues, I started to listen to some fusion stuff like Jaco, John Scofield, etc. It really turned my head. I was definitely hooked on the jazz stuff and really got into the Charlie Parker and Miles Davis tradition. This definitely drove me to take up the upright bass and led me to becoming a more full-time player. I believe playing cello helped with my initial studies on the upright bass. Unfortunately, my studies on the cello were obscured by sports and other distractions . . . I left the instrument by tenth grade.

(JC) Can you discuss how you manage to survive as a working bassist in today's world with a declining economy and people having less money to spend on the arts?

(JM) There is so much working against today's musician. I don't think I need to discuss all the negatives associated with this business. Between the economy and the ignorance of the public, today's musician is climbing up hill for certain. If you tell the average person in our society that you're a full-time musician, they look at you as if you have two heads and ask you, "What's the name of your band?" You have to have a good attitude and an open mind to survive. I try to balance my schedule with a lot of different types of gigs, some pay well and others hardly pay. For instance, I play about forty to fifty weddings a year, plus private party stuff I pick-up myself. I also keep busy with a stream of steady local bar and restaurant gigs. Some of these gigs I have been playing for many years. These steady gigs have helped me hone in on my chops, learn repertoire (mostly jazz standards), meet great local musicians, and just be present on the scene to establish other work. You need to stay focused on being creative, which is the core reason why someone decides to be a full-time musician, but realize you need to make a living. I think today's definition of a full-time musician is someone who has decided to make music a main focus in his/her life. There are some full-time public school music teachers that I would consider full-time players, just because of their level of commitment to their craft.

(JC) Can you describe what you believe is essential, regarding both personality and politics, when aspiring to be a full time bassist?

(JM) I truly believe having a good attitude and personality is important in music. With that said, having confidence is even more important. I have definitely found myself in playing situations that were way over my head. It's taken me many years to hone in on the art of remaining confident and getting through a tough musical situation . . . Especially for someone like me, who has chosen to play a difficult genre of music and never attended music school. It's important to push myself even if it means falling down sometimes. I've probably been not called back for certain gigs because it didn't go well, but sometimes you have to think of the long-term and get the experience so you can cut these difficult gigs. Having confidence and not being afraid of challenging situations is most important.

(JC) Where do you go to check out jazz when you have a night off and why? Who or what has inspired you musically?

(JM) I'm one of those musicians who almost enjoys listening to music as much as performing it. There is so much you can pick-up from watching other bassists and musicians perform, especially with the upright bass. More than the notes which become a blur by the next day, the attitude, posture and relaxation of the player or players can have a profound effect on your playing and approach to the instrument. I mostly go to the smaller jazz clubs such as the Zinc Bar or 55 Bar, but if there is somebody I really want to hear like Dave Holland or Gonzales Rubbacatta, I will go to a bigger club and pay the higher cost. I have been inspired by so many musicians and styles of music it would take up the whole page. I pretty much can be inspired by any genre of music, if it speaks to me. When performing, I enjoy working with all different styles of musicians as long as it "clicks." I did study for a couple of years with a great upright bass player named Bill McCrossen who really inspired me and gave me the direction I needed when I first started playing. Good teachers really make a difference . . .

(JC) This is a two-part question: What basses and amps are you currently using? And how do you deal with young, beautiful groupies rushing the stage night after night?

(JM) I have an old German carved wood bass which is my main axe. I don't rely heavily on the amp for volume when it comes to upright bass, so I try to get as much sound acoustically possible out of the bass. I do have a small Acoustic Image amplifier, which I plug into with a small mic. I have a Fishman full circle pick-up installed on the bass which I can use if it's a loud musical setting, but I really don't like the sound of any pickup. My bass is strung with Velvet Anima strings which I've been using for a few years now. They're great if you want to hit hard with the right hand. I have been playing a lot of electric bass lately and I've always used Fender. I have a Jazz fretted, Precision fretted and a fretless, all of which are four strings. I power the electric basses through a Walter Woods 300 watt amplifier and two BrickHouse speakers with ten and twelve inch woofers.

And I suppose there are a few groupies here and there . . .

www.MySpace.com/JerryMcDonaldMusic
www.JerryMcDonaldMusic.com

Bassist: Jerry McDonald
Interviewed by: John Carey

www.JohnCarey.net

Photo by Vanessa Eaton

Interview with NYC bassist, Chris Tarry:

Chris Tarry is a professional bassist in New York City since 2003, originally from Canada. He is successful as a sideman, producer, and as an artist, composing and producing his own records as well. Chris has worked with John Scofield, Bill Evans, Ben Monder, Mino Cinelu, Dave Binney, Jim Rotondi Group, Keith Carlock, Anton Fig, Donny McCaslin, Lew Soloff, Chris Cheek, Oz Noy Trio, Gene Jackson, DJ Logic and many others.

(JC) As a somewhat recent "transplant," can you discuss what the transition to NYC was like, specifically in the beginning?

(CT) Well, my transition to New York was a pretty up and down one as I would assume most are. I was leaving a very successful career in Canada. While in Canada I was getting a lot of calls to play on people's electric jazz albums . . . calls where they wanted "me for me" and to do "what I did," whatever that was. I was very fortunate. That's a place most people strive their whole career to get to.

In 2002, I had just come out of a long term relationship and for a time I considered doing something completely different: business, cop, real estate, etc. It was an interesting spot to be in, to look over the edge of a successful musical career and not care whether you ever play another note again. I told myself that I had to give it one more "kick at-the-can." I had spent so much time practicing and playing over the years, I had to give it another shot, and what better place to do that than in New York. So I packed up everything I owned, sold the rest, and literally arrived in New York with a suitcase, a practice amp and a bass. I rented a little apartment in Brooklyn from a friend I met on CraigsList and that was it. I was in New York.

It was a hard start, I came from a place where most people knew who I was; I had to start from the beginning. For a few years after arriving I would ask myself the same daily question, "If I knew what I know now about New York, how hard it is here, would I do it again?" The answer until only about two years ago was always, "No." It was hard.

The interesting thing was that it always seemed that when things were at their worst, no gigs and bartending to make a little extra money, something would pop up. I have this one moment forever etched into my head . . . I was walking home from bar tending another fifteen hour shift. I had been here for about six months, things were slow, and my good friend, the famous Canadian impresario Cory Weeds, had just been in for a visit. He saw I was struggling and mentioned me to the great New York trumpet player, Jim Rotondi. Jim called me out of the blue after hearing a CD that Cory had given him and hired me for his electric band. That was the turning point. That one phone call made me stay. I've since relayed that story to Jim and he doesn't really believe me. It's funny, I can think back to my coming to New York and every time it's just a few names that pop up that really helped me out: the same people time and time again that believed in me.

(JC) How did the music scene here in New York compare to the scene in Canada?

(CT) Well, like I said I was known back in Canada as a top call, high-end kinda electric jazz dude. I had to get my side man chops together pretty quickly when I moved here, not that I didn't play any other music. I was one of the busiest guys in Vancouver before I left, playing studio sessions, lots of R&B, singer songwriters, but I never really focused on it and when

I arrived here it showed, at least to me. I knuckled down and didn't write any of my own music for a few years or really focus on my own group. I just did gigs, anything and everything. I taped myself all the time, tried to learn and started playing with certain people that helped me focus on various micro nuances in certain styles. I worked on my reading, bought a P bass and started to play that exclusively. It was more intense here, less room for error, and you needed to be "on" all the time, so I worked to try and make that happen.

(JC) Because of the recent success with your own record release, *Almost Certainly Dreaming* (2008 Juno Award), many people recognize you as a jazz and fusion bassist and composer. Can you discuss the importance of playing all kinds of music in order to make a living here in NYC?

(CT) You gotta be able to do it all, the good, the bad, and the ugly. I will honestly say that I have played some of the greatest music I will ever play right here in New York. But, especially in the beginning, I also played some of the worst. It's a big place. You gotta learn to do every kind of gig and try and learn from them all. Now, that doesn't mean you're always the right guy for every gig either, no matter how good of a side man you are. You learn pretty quickly how to not take things personally when working in this town. They can be onto the sixth bass player on the list before you even know you've been fired! There's no crying in New York.

(JC) Do you find that it's difficult to not get categorized as a "jazz bassist" when seeking work within the singer-songwriter scene? How do you maintain both identities?

(CT) I'm really lucky; people just seem to call now. I guess I have enough of a foot in different scenes that at least one or two of the feet are usually dancing at any given time. That said, I really try and keep all the different "scenes" completely separate. I have a strict "no jazz talk" policy with any of the pop people I work with, and I use specific types of basses for different types of gigs. If I've been working for a certain artist for a long time and we're good friends they'll eventually find out about my own career as a jazz artist, but as a rule, never the two shall meet. It took me a long time to figure all that out. It takes a lot of self control and realizing that 99.9% of all gigs are not about you. The sooner you learn that in New York the sooner you'll be making a living here.

(JC) How important to you is being a good reader? What type of gigs want you to read and how often do you get a reading gig?

(CT) If you want to work a lot in many different situations you need to be able to read well. On a basic level reading a chord chart is totally essential. Being able to read bass lines is the next level up from that and also important. A lot of times I'll be on gigs where there are no chords, just a line, that's the toughest, and again, pretty important to be able to do well. I find actually the more commercial stuff I do requires a lot of reading (club dates [wedding bands], studio jingles, etc.). You *will* be asked to read. I get some of my most challenging reading in people's original jazz projects that I'm asked to play in. That stuff is usually crazy hard and most leaders know to get ya the charts ahead of time so there's time to practice it before the gig.

www.ChrisTarry.com
www.MySpace.com/ChrisTarry

Bassist: Chris Tarry
Interviewed by: John Carey

www.JohnCarey.net

Interview with NYC/NJ bassist, Bailey Gee:

Bailey Gee is a professional bassist in Northern New Jersey. He is a self-taught bassist, and he later studied at Kean University in NJ. Bailey has worked extensively with drum legend, Bernard Purdie, as well as with the Hudson River Rats (featuring harmonica virtuoso Rob Paparozzi). He recently opened for Roberta Flack as part of a "dream band" that featured Bernard Purdie and legends Lou Marini, Tom Malone, Leon Pendarvis, Steve Cropper, George Naha, John Korba, Rob Paparozzi and Eddie Floyd. Bailey has performed at numerous educational and drum clinics with Bernard, as well as appearing with him at the Modern Drummer Festival. He recently cut rhythm tracks with him (and *SNL* band's Shawn Pelton) for Rob Paparozzi's new CD release. Bailey is a founding member of jazz group, Soulminded, and he co-produced the group's first CD release, *Power of the Flock*, featuring BS&T and Ween keyboardist, Glenn McClelland, Angelo Dibraccio on sax and Dave Mohn on drums. In addition, he has backed such entertainers such as Red Buttons, Connie Stevens and David Brenner.

(JC) You are known as a groove player. Who were some of your main influences and what songs or grooves in particular have helped to influence your style of playing the most?

(BG) Chuck Rainey, James Jamerson, Rocco Prestia, Jerry Jemmott, Jaco, Will Lee and Marcus Miller were some notable electric bass inspirations, and I worked to cop some of their grooves and licks. Ray Brown, Ron Carter and Buster Williams were some upright players I paid attention to. I was always attracted to players who focused more on groove and song support. I noticed early on that although these players all played similar simple instruments, they all had a unique sound and a style that was their own. This made me realize how true Jaco's comments were that your sound comes from your hands and head.

But more important, and to me more fascinating, is the larger part of my playing style that I did not consciously "work on" that emerged somehow via osmosis from extensive listening to classic blues, soul, R&B, funk and jazz records. You may not even know who the bassists were, but the styles, phrasing, and grooves enter your subconscious and unintentionally become a part of your overall approach and style. Extensive listening to genres of music you are interested in playing is essential in my opinion.

(JC) How have you seen the music business change over the years? As a sideman, how has it affected work for you?

(BG) Years ago I realized that a singing bassist had an edge and often got hired over a non-singing player. So early on I made a point of working on background vocals, harmonies and eventually lead vocals, as well as my bass playing. This has been a big asset in terms of staying employed, and I have been hired on numerous gigs that had specified "vocals a big plus" or "must sing lead/backing vocals." I enjoy the challenge of maintaining a tight bass groove while singing.

In the mid eighties and early nineties, many bassists shifted to an extremely bright tone, and were commonly replaced with fatter sounding keyboard synth bass patches. I am happy to see the trend these days is again towards bass guitar with a fuller and more vintage sounding bass tone (and flatwound strings are more commonly being used).

In recent years, we've all seen the NYC area live music club scene diminish, and some of my favorite venues to play (like La Bar Bat) are no longer around. The popularity of DJ's has also had an effect on the club scene, as well as club dates (weddings, corporate events, etc.), and they have reduced the amount of work available to a NYC gigging musician. On the plus side, high quality home recording equipment has become much more affordable, and this has opened many new opportunities and paid situations for working bassists.

(JC) Can you discuss what it is like to work with the legendary Bernard Purdie?

(BG) Playing with Bernard is a pleasure, and I constantly have bassists telling me that it would be their dream gig. Bernard is so groove-oriented and song-oriented. Everything about what he does is to support and lift the song.

I had been listening to records with Bernard on drums (along with Chuck Rainey and Jerry Jemmott on bass) ever since I was young and starting to play bass. So when I first had the opportunity to work with him, I found it extremely easy to connect with him and instinctively knew how to lock into his grooves. Later, when doing drum clinics with him and attempting to explain and demonstrate the bass/drum relationship, I began to recognize and identify some of these concepts that came to me instinctively, such as intentionally playing behind or ahead of the beat, beat subdivision, and enhancing rhythms using ghosting techniques.

(JC) You have been a professional bassist for over thirty-five years, and you are one of many who have decided to get a day job. Can you discuss why you went this route?

(BG) I was a successful full-time musician for many years, but at some point I became frustrated and tired of playing material and playing in situations where my heart was not into it in order to stay afloat financially.

When I started getting calls from some big name players that I wanted to work with, I decided I didn't want to have to turn down these opportunities because I was afraid to lose my unrewarding "steady money" gig. So I got some computer training and now work during the day as a consulting software developer. It is a flexible enough situation to allow days off for recording and short road tours, and still lets me maintain a fairly busy NYC area gigging schedule with artists I enjoy and choose to work with.

(JC) Which basses are your main live and recording axes?

(BG) When I started playing professionally, I played Fender Precision and Jazz basses. Fender had very little true competition in those days in regard to tone and playability. Then for about ten to fifteen years I was on a five string quest and owned and played five strings by almost every major custom builder.

These days I prefer to play my old four string vintage passive Fenders again. I have two Precisions and two Jazz basses in my regular rotation (one each with flats and one with rounds). When a five string is appropriate, I use my Fodera Emperor five or an Alleva-Coppola jazz-style five string. On acoustic and jazzy gigs, I'll sometimes play my Rob Allen semi-acoustic or Tacoma Thunderchief ABG with black nylon strings, or an Azola Baby Bass EUB. I also recently acquired a beautiful and tuneful Kolstein Busetto upright travel bass that I am using quite a bit lately on various gigs and recordings.

But if I could have only one, my hands-down desert island bass would be a pre-CBS Precision strung with LaBella flats, but with a set of Rotosound roundwound strings tucked in the case for good measure.

Bassist: Bailey Gee
Interviewed by: John Carey

www.JohnCarey.net

Interview with NYC bassist, Brian Killeen:

Brian Killeen is a professional electric and upright bassist in New York City. He is bass player for The Josh Dion Band, and he has toured extensively with guitarist/composer, Chuck Loeb. Brian studied bass privately with Avishai Cohen. Avishai later sought Brian for several bass duets at New York shows, including performances at Birdland, Blue Note and Smalls. In addition, he spent most of his four years at William Paterson University studying and performing on acoustic bass. In his senior year at WPU, he and drummer Josh Dion joined established NYC funk/jam outfit ulu. Later, in 2005, Brian joined drummer Josh Dion in guitarist/composer Chuck Loeb's band. With Loeb, he toured throughout the States and internationally, while meeting/performing with musicians Will Lee, Randy Brecker and Bob James. The Josh Dion Band releases their new album, *Anthems*, for the Long Distance in 2008. Brian is also a freelance bassist on both electric and upright bass for several artists and bands.

(JC) Can you discuss your experiences as a student at William Paterson University? Do you feel it necessary to have a formal education in order to be a working bassist here in New York City?

(BK) I happened to attend William Paterson at an extremely fertile time. The amazing Rufus Reid had run the program up until I entered in the fall of '99. So while the jazz program itself was in a transitional phase, the relatively small base of students immediately bonded and formed a tight-knit unit, both musically and socially. All members of the Josh Dion Band happened to meet and gig together during this time. I do not believe it is at all necessary to have a formal education in order to be a working NYC bassist. Knowledge of theory, reading and history can all be acquired via private teachers and self-study. The invaluable things that an institution can provide are constant exposure to like-minded individuals and teachers, performance opportunities, and in the case of William Paterson, proximity to the greatest music city in the world.

(JC) Originally from Long Island, you've spent most of your life right here in New York. How would you describe the music scene in its current state with regard to getting work as a sideman? What are some of the ways you go about getting gigs?

(BK) I would say that, in my observations at least, there are currently many opportunities for work as a sideman in NYC. I will say that the work can be a bit clustered and "clique-ish", though. It is beneficial to find a "scene" or a group of artists you'd like to work with and, without being pushy, let them know who you are and what you're there to do. While I never made a conscious effort at networking, what has helped me get gigs is associating myself with people who inspire me both musically and personally. Through that, the opportunities have presented themselves in such a way that I rarely do a gig I don't enjoy.

(JC) Are there any bassists you look up to or take guidance from (musically or music business related)? What bassists in New York inspire you to continue playing and keep you motivated as a player?

(BK) I try to look to everyone for guidance. There is always something to be learned from someone's experiences, be it the right or wrong way to do things. That is what is great about the NYC bass brunch. You have bassists from all walks of life and fields under the same roof. You can gain insight regarding the Broadway scene, studio work, gear, etc. The three bassists I have taken the most guidance from are Avishai Cohen, Will Lee and Mike Visceglia. Avishai provided me with my first epiphany for upright bass and later took me under his wing, helping me select a bass and develop a complete sound. Mike and Will, to me, are the quintessential NYC working bassists. They are always dispelling some kind of wisdom or hilarious story (not to mention amazingly musical bass lines). With or without a bass on, any room they step into benefits from their presence. Some of my other favorite NYC bassists are Tim Lefebvre, Nicholas D'Amato, Brett Bass and plenty others that I'll probably think of after this interview . . .

(JC) Can you share some of your experiences working with Chuck Loeb?

(BK) With all the horror stories you hear in the music industry, I am very proud to admit that I have absolutely nothing but great things to say about Chuck. In the three years in his band, I have learned what it is to be a true professional. He leads a band with a healthy mix of discipline and camaraderie that helps make the music come to life. He encourages each player in the band to serve the music strongly while also having time to stretch out and showcase their individual musical personality. I also learned to build my chops up playing all those band unison lines at the finales of the sets! The core band, including Josh Dion on drums and Matt King on keys, are non-stop hilarity on the road. One of the more hysterical moments was when Matt decided to take on the Northern Spain tradition of pouring the region's indigenous cider (usually designated for a trained waiter) into multiple glasses with pouring hand raised high above one's head. What resulted was very little cider in the glasses and many confused onlookers.

(JC) If you could only choose five attributes (musically or personally) that a bassist must have in order to be a working bassist here in New York, what would they be?

(BK)
1. As The Rock would say, "KNOW YOUR ROLE!" If you're looking to do jazz work, know your standards! If you want to do studio/theater work, get your reading chops up. If you're playing with singers/bands, know how to make *them* sound good!

2) HAVE ALL "BASSES" COVERED (couldn't resist the pun): Have the right instrument(s) for the line of work you want to do. If you're primarily doing singer/songwriter work, ditch the six string piece of "furniture" and grab the Fender. Just the same, maybe the vintage P bass isn't the ideal axe for your Balkan fusion group (or maybe it is?).

3) HUMILITY: Check your ego at the door, ask questions and remember that as a sideman, you are there to serve the situation, not yourself.

4) BE PERSONABLE: Look at your favorite working bassists. You won't see them showing up angry and drunk to the gigs. People are hiring you not only to fit the bill musically, but to show up on time, be prepared and create a comfortable situation ideal for music-making.

5) HAVE FUN! That is why we started playing in the first place, right?

www.MySpace.com/RocknRollBrian

Bassist: Brian Killeen
Interviewed by: John Carey

www.JohnCarey.net

Photo by David Sokol

Interview with NYC bassist, Mike Visceglia:

Mike Visceglia is a professional bassist and sideman, music director, producer and bass columnist. He has worked with John Cale, Suzanne Vega, Shawn Colvin, Dar Williams, Bette Midler, Phil Collins, Bruce Springsteen, Pete Seeger, Phoebe Snow, Al Green, Michelle Shocked, Jackson Browne and Valerie Carter, to name a few. He is also author of *A View from the Side*, which includes interviews with many top bassists worldwide as well as many of his own road worthy stories.

(JC) You have become a prominent figure within the bass community, eager to lend truthful and thoughtful advice to new bassists hitting the New York scene. How do you go about ensuring that you will have a consistent work flow? What are some ways that you generating work, either as bassist, music director or producer?

(MV) I have the advantage of being born and raised in NYC and the surrounding areas. After so many years of being on the scene and playing and studying, I've developed a reputation in the community as someone who is not only very capable, but willing to offer my skills, experience and advice to any artists who hire me. But in NY you can never rest or be complacent. There are lots of great players out there and your networking ability, people skills and tenacity have to go hand in hand with your playing. Today it's especially important to be diverse and cultivate as many skills as possible, be it anything related to the bass or studio production, arranging or Internet skills. That's what will give you the best chances to keep work flowing.

(JC) You've described the current state of the music business to be in "flux." Can you elaborate on this and describe how it affects those of us performing as sidemen?

(MV) One cannot conceptualize the business today as it once was. Large studios are going out of business daily and record companies have changed dramatically. Money is tighter and salaries in general aren't what they once were. The way to record and distribute music is profoundly different than any previous time. The age of the professional studio musician has waned. The up side to this is that there are more live opportunities for sidemen as artists, and bands need to go on tour more to generate income through performing and merchandise sales to make up for the drop in CD sales. There are also a plethora of small studios and independent artists committed to making records (as that is easier than ever to do). There are great opportunities for forward thinking entrepreneurs to come up with a better paradigm for creating business in the music industry. Independent minded artists and businessmen will survive. As I stated in the previous question, diversity is key. Let's add self sufficiency and ingenuity to that. Those are the musicians who will survive the "flux."

(JC) What things outside of the realm of music help you "regenerate" and allow for a balance within your busy schedule?

(MV) I am very into movies and books. They keep me intellectually stimulated and refreshed. I'm also thankful for a supportive wife and the most soulful dog on the planet, Jasper. They keep me grounded.

(JC) What advice can you give to bassists who are already great bassists and musicians, but are seeking higher profile artists to work with?

(MV) New York is the biggest showcase in the world. Go out and play as much as possible. Even the most inconspicuous venue or gig can be a stepping stone to your dream gig. You never know who's watching you at a NYC gig. If you don't live in NY and you're driven to be a player with world class success, I suggest that you move to a place where there is a world class scene. Go out and study other successful bassists. Try to understand what it is that makes them successful. Get your personal and professional skills in tip top shape.

(JC) Is it important in the New York scene to have an image, and if so, how important is it in relation to being a good player? Is image more important for upcoming players in the NYC scene than it is for established bassists?

(MV) I think image is very important *but* there are two ways of looking at it. If you're going after a big pop gig, then how you look is going to be as important as your playing. If you're going after a great musical gig how you "are" is going to be as important as your playing. By that I mean how your vibe is, how you carry yourself and comport with other players, how confident and good humored you are. All of this is image to me and it does matter.

www.MikeVisceglia.com

Bassist: Mike Visceglia
Interviewed by: John Carey

www.JohnCarey.net

Interview with NYC luthier, Roger Sadowsky:

In 1979 **Roger Sadowsky** opened up his own shop in New York City where he quickly became famous for guitar and bass guitar repair and instrument building. Bass greats such as Marcus Miller and Will Lee helped to spread the work of Roger's fantastic craftsmanship. In addition, Roger's bass guitar preamp became world renowned and bassists throughout the metro area and across the globe began to upgrade their basses with his inboard and outboard preamp. Today, many top musicians continue to rely on Roger's instruments for both studio and live work; such bassists include Tal Wilkenfeld, Chris Chaney, Tim Lefebvre, Mickey Madden and the list goes on. Roger has mastered the skill of creating instruments that are lightweight, aesthetically stunning, tonally unprecedented and wonderful to play, without compromising that warm and inviting tone that one might assume only heavier vintage basses could provide.

(JC) Many different types of bass players from NYC and around the world have chosen to use your guitars and basses as their main instruments for both studio and live work. If you had to choose only five attributes that most players want from their instruments (specifically for the bass guitar), what would they be?

(RS) The top three have always been:
1. Sounds good.
2. Feels good.
3. Looks good.

If I had to add two more, it would be:
4. Cuts through good.
5. Reliable and dependable.

(JC) How have your basses changed since you began building in the early 1980s? Why were these changes made?

(RS) I think the biggest change was adding five strings in the early nineties. I was initially resistant to them, but I finally saw the light. But I draw the line at five strings. There will be no six string Sadowsky basses. I also think, that among the so called "boutique builders" I probably still make and sell more four string basses than anyone else.

The other biggest change was going to a chambered body, which we started a few years ago. I was always into light weight and acoustically resonant basses. I noticed that over the years, the body woods from my wood suppliers (ash and alder) were getting progressively heavier. I began to chamber my bodies to keep the weight down. But everyone began to comment on how much better they thought the basses were sounding with the chambered bodies.

(JC) Many of the basses that you offer are based on standard Jazz and Precision basses, but offer many "improvements" on Fender's original designs. How does the recent shift of interest back towards vintage basses affect your business? Or, because vintage instruments are currently so expensive, do you notice any affect on business at all?

(RS) The vintage scene has influenced me to make some "Ultra-Vintage" models, which is our interpretation of a vintage Fender. Full size bodies, more radius in the fingerboard, Brazilian rosewood fingerboards, single coil pickups . . . something for the working musician to get as close to a vintage Fender as possible, but with the Sadowsky improvements, and at a fraction of the cost of vintage Fenders today. No one wants to take a $20,000 bass on a gig.

(JC) Why do you feel that the Jazz and Precision bass have become an essential part of the working bassist's "toolbox?" Is it because we take comfort in the familiar or is it because they are truly the best sounding and playing basses available?

(RS) First is history. The 802 Union directories in the 70s had two categories for bass: Acoustic Bass and Fender Bass. When I started building in the very early 80s, the studio players felt a lot of pressure to show up with a Fender bass. There was a lot of jingle work at that time and these were short forty-five minute sessions. The engineers knew how to get a good sound from a Fender in a matter of seconds. There was no time to spend ten minutes trying to dial in an unfamiliar bass on the board.

So as much as I would have liked to build a more original style bass, I felt a pressure to build within the Fender paradigm. It certainly doesn't hurt that Leo pretty much nailed it. I really do not think there is anything else out there that is superior to the basic Fender J and P design.

(JC) Building the instruments that so many players are using must provide you with a sense of responsibility combined with a sense of accomplishment and pride. Is this what inspires you to build basses or does the source of your inspiration come elsewhere?

(RS) I am very proud of what I have accomplished over the last thirty-six years of instrument making. But my inspiration comes from my desire to make a contribution to people's lives. Instrument making is the way I do it, but it is not about the bass or the guitar itself. It is about the person ordering and purchasing the instrument. It is about listening to what people want and need and doing my best to give it to them. It is about providing them with the highest level of customer service that I can. That is the main reason I always kept my business at a size where I could deal directly with the player, rather than with the purchasing agent for a chain of music stores.

The reward is getting emails from people all over the world, telling me how much they love my instruments and dealing with my staff. A bass is an inanimate object— there is no inherent satisfaction that comes from making them independent of the player.

www.Sadowsky.com

Luthier: Roger Sadowsky
Interviewed by: John Carey

www.JohnCarey.net

Photo by Annalee Van Kleek

Interview with NYC bassist, Irio O'Farrill:

Irio O'Farrill is one of the leading bassists in the New York City music scene. He earned a B.A. in music from New Jersey City University and later went to Manhattan School of Music and New York University. Irio has worked with Juan Carlos Formell, Bobby Sanabria and Ascención, the Chico O'Farrill Afro-Cuban Jazz Orchestra, Gary Morgan and Pan Americana, Dave Valentin, Ray Mantilla and Space Station, Daniel Ponce, Claudio Roditi, Steve Turre, Los Jovenes Del Barrio, The Dalton Gang, The Real Deal Big Band, Larry Gatlin, BeBe Winans, Laurie Beechman, Sarah Brightman and many others. His Broadway credits include *Cats, Grease, Footloose, The Rocky Horror Show, Hairspray, Brooklyn the Musical, The Wedding Singer* and the Latin-Hip Hop show, *In the Heights*. In 2006, Irio was part of the JCS All Star Band for *Jesus Christ Superstar*: Live In Concert in Hollywood, CA, featuring Ted Neely, Yvonne Elliman, Ben Vereen, Clint Holmes and Jack Black. He is a faculty member of the Bass Collective, The New School for Jazz and Contemporary Music and Stevens Institute of Technology. Irio is a co-author of the recently released instructional book, *Afro-Caribbean & Brazilian Rhythms for the Bass*, published by Carl Fischer.

(JC) What is the most common area of weakness that you come across in bass students?

(IO) Probably the most common weakness I see is that students can't read. It's a given that you have to have good ears and good time and feel, among other things, to be a good bass player. I think a lot of players are limiting themselves work wise because they can't read.

(JC) If you had to choose five attributes that a bassist must have in order to become and remain a working bassist in NYC, what would they be?

1. (IO) 1. Good basic musicianship. All the things I mentioned above and more.

2. Versatility. Be able to play or at least have some knowledge of several different styles.

3. Being able to play both electric and acoustic bass (something I wish I could do better). The way the business is now, I think it's really become a necessity.

4. Have good networking skills and some business sense.

5. Have a good attitude and perseverance.

(JC) How difficult is it for a bassist to break into the Broadway scene, and what might you suggest if someone were interested in finding this kind of work?

(IO) Because there isn't much studio work in New York anymore, Broadway has now become one of the best steady gigs in town, which means you're competing for work with some of the best players in town. As with anything in this business, it's all about who you know. Getting to know players that have shows and subbing for them is the way to break in. I subbed for years before I ever got my own show. For younger players, studying with guys that have shows could help. I now have two former students subbing for me.

(JC) How imperative do you feel getting a formal education in music is, specifically for bass? Can you be a successful bassist in NYC without it?

(IO) I think it depends on the individual and what your goals are. There is a lot to be gained from going to school. I would definitely recommend it, but it's not for everyone. There are plenty of great and successful players in town that don't have a formal education.

(JC) Is there a common personality trait that you can see in those bassists who are able to remain working in New York?

(IO) The great thing about bass players in New York is that we're all respectful of what we do and of each other. Our role as bass players is primarily a supportive one. I think we tend to be supportive of each other and that's what keeps us working.

www.MySpace.com/IrioOFarrill

Bassist: Irio O'Farrill
Interviewed by: John Carey

www.JohnCarey.net

Interview with NYC bassist, Meshell Ndegéocello:

Meshell Ndegéocello is a bassist, singer and songwriter in New York City. Born in Germany, Meshell and her family moved to Virginia in the early 1970s. Meshell began to perform regularly in the Washington D.C. area before coming to New York City to reside and to work as a bass player. She briefly studied music at Howard University. In the early 1990s, Meshell joined with Madonna's record label, Maverick, to pursue her solo career. In addition, she has worked with John Mellencamp, Chaka Khan, Mike Stern, Joshua Redman, Alanis Morissette, Santana, Joan Osborne, Indigo Girls, Sarah McLachlan, David Sanborn, The Rolling Stones, Marcus Miller and Steve Coleman, to name a very few.

(JC) When did you first come to New York City to pursue music, and what were your original impressions of the music scene in NYC at that time?

(MN) I came when I was twenty…1998. I thought the scene was alive and thriving. There was always somewhere to play and always somewhere to hear something.

(JC) What were some of the first gigs you picked up in NYC and how did you go about seeking work as a bassist when you first arrived?

(MN) Bill Toles managed this group I played with in DC. When I first got here, I stayed with him. He was having his house replastered by Craig Street. Craig and Bill worked with the Black Rock Coalition . . . Craig was putting together a Hendrix tribute and Bill conducted the BRC Orchestra. They hooked me up with gigs.

(JC) How has the music scene changed in NYC since you have been here with regard to getting work as a sideman and for performing your own original music?

(MN) There are a lot of jam band gigs and cover band gigs but I don't think I'd fare well if I were getting here now. I'd have to play a five string and have a huge catalog of tunes in my head. I've been lucky in playing my own music, but it's not easy.

(JC) What other artists do you currently enjoy sitting in with?

(MN) I like to sit in with Jason Lindner. I have to say I'm not really the sit-in type. I like to rehearse and learn the music and play things to the best of my ability. I'm not the quickest learner but I have a vast imagination. I feel like I can approach the bass line as if it were a song; I never wanted to be a rip and run soloist. I'm a fluffer . . . the moodsetter.

(JC) What advice would you give bassists in NYC who are already competent bass players but are seeking work with higher profile artists?

(MN) I believe so much of it is being in the right place at the right time. Keep your ear to the ground. Be able to communicate with the artist and play the way they hear it. Know your schedule. Get a contract. Just keep yourself together. It's an ever-changing business. Personally, I'm at the end of that. I want gigs that are challenging, or that give me a creative outlet. Often, with high profile gigs you lose the opportunities to really *play*.

www.FreeMyHeart.com

Bassist: Meshell Ndegéocello
Interviewed by: John Carey

www.JohnCarey.net

Photo by Melissa Clark

Interview with Chicago/NYC bassist, John Abbey:

John Abbey is an upright and electric bassist and producer, originally from NYC but currently located in Chicago. He has worked with David Poe, Block, John Cale, Ray Davies, Hubert Sumlin, Daniel Lanois, Mark Geary, Amy Speace, Janet Bean, Carolyne Mas, Neal Casal, Dog's Eye View, Bobby Sichran, Mike Errico, Stacie Rose, Alex Forbes, Amanda Thorpe, Todd Kray, Karen Novy, Barbara Brousal, Dan Zanes and Robbie Fulks, to name a few.

(JC) How long have you been playing bass and who/what turned you on to the instrument?

(JA) I've been playing bass since the last Yankee dynasty, or thereabouts. It wasn't any big "calling" to play really. One summer my friends and I would hang out at my house every morning and listen to records and play air guitar. It was probably 1975/76. It was a lot of The Yes album, Hot Tuna, *Burgers* (Jack Casady one my all time favorites), Cream, *Disralei Gears*, Jimi Hendrix, *Smash Hits*, The Who, *Tommy* . . . I could keep going! What a fun summer it was discovering all that stuff.

My older brother played bass. He was left handed and I assumed so was his instrument. On one particularly animated air guitar session, I decided to play "air bass" with my brother's instrument. When I opened up the case and picked it up I was delighted to find that it was right handed. My brother learned to play upside down! That was it for me and I haven't stopped since. (By the way, his bass was a cherry red Guild Starfire, single pickup.)

(JC) Can you discuss what it's like playing both upright bass and electric bass? What are the advantages/disadvantages, and is it challenging to maintain adequacy on both instruments?

(JA) As my ability progressed on electric bass I was looking for "harder" stuff to play. I got into Weather Report, Return to Forever, Stanley Clarke, Billy Cobham and anything with Marcus Miller. I was learning all my "jazz heads" trying to play *Donna Lee* like Jaco, etc. I was also listening to Miles Davis, John Coltrane, Dexter Gordon, Sonny Rollins and Charlie Parker. I decided that if I was going to play jazz, I'd play it on upright. I got a plywood Juzek and I got myself ready to practice. I tried learning the "technique" and immediately abandoned it. The upright sat in the corner for a couple of years. In order to not lose a gig when a singer-songwriter asked for upright, I'd tell them, "Yeah, no problem, I'll do your gig on upright." It forced me to learn how to play *bass*, not jazz. My facility on upright was non existent. It made me think a lot more about what I was going to play. That economic approach infiltrated my electric playing, making me realize that I didn't need all those notes to say something.

I don't think there are any disadvantages of playing both. You'll work more and if you're open musically, each one is going to influence the other. For me, if I'm not playing a lot of upright for a period of time my stamina diminishes. Sometimes that ain't a bad thing . . . makes me think, "Do I really need to do that?"

(JC) What are you listening to at the moment for enjoyment and/or inspiration?

(JA) I've been all over the map recently, rediscovering Big Star and all the Sly and The Family Stone stuff. *Mule Variations* by Tom Waits, *Milestones* by Miles Davis, loving the *Juno* soundtrack, Sharon Jones and the Dap Kings. My nine year old has gotten me into Beyonce, Fergie and Alicia keys . . . Air America Radio.

(JC) What instruments are you using as your main axes for live and recording purposes? What attributes do you want, need and expect from a bass in general? Do you have a string preference?

(JA) My main electrics are a 1966 Fender Jazz bass and a late 60s Vox Violin Bass (Bill Wyman model). My upright is a carved copy of a flat-back Fendt by Barrie Kolstein. I like and want basses to sound and feel good (I know, I'm stating the obvious). I forget where I heard it but it seems true: "If a bass sounds good unplugged, it'll sound good when plugged in." I don't want the neck to "move" and need to be set up frequently. I'm not a huge fan of on board pre-amps and active electronics, although sometimes I do want it for that modern sound. Both my electrics are strung with LaBella flatwounds. The Fender is strung heavy, Vox a bit lighter . . . kind of "old school." I haven't changed them in years. I'm embarrassed to say I don't even know what's on my upright (sorry Barrie).

(JC) I understand that you are also producing records in addition to being a "bassist for hire." Can you discuss what services you offer clients and how they can contact you if they are interested in working with you?

(JA) I started producing some records in NY and learning my engineering chops "on the gig." I then moved to Chicago in 2002. Fortunately the engineering/producing side of things has followed me here and it has continued to grow. People aren't working with me because I have gear . . . everyone has gear. I think bassists in general are the mediators, both musically and personally in most bands, straddling the line between rhythm and harmony, bridging all the proverbial gaps between personalities, and maintaining the calm amongst a guitar riff and drum fill-filled world. Or maybe it's because I have gear.

www.MySpace.com/JohnAbbeySoup
www.JohnAbbey.com
www.ESession.com/JohnAbbey

Bassist: John Abbey
Interviewed by: John Carey

www.JohnCarey.net

Photo by Andrea Scher

Interview with NYC bassist, Malcolm Gold:

Malcolm Gold is a bassist living in New York City. He studied at Berklee College of Music in Boston, MA. He has worked with Sheryl Crow, the Tony award winning production *Movin' Out*, Trans-Siberian Orchestra, Morgan Heritage, Dan Zanes, G.E. Smith, Days of the New, India.Arie and many others.

(JC) Do you feel that a formal music education is mandatory in order to be a working bassist here in New York City?

(MG) I don't think there are any set rules to it, but it has certainly helped me. Reading music, for example, is something that has proven very valuable to me throughout my life. In a town like NYC, where everything moves fast and people are usually very busy, being able to read music saves a lot of time, which in turn saves producers and artists money. On the other hand, there is something to be said for having great ears and instincts. Formal training may put you on the right path, but it will never give you what actual working, playing or listening experience will.

(JC) What can you recommend to players who are in New York and are looking for work with higher profile artists?

(MG) I don't think it's any different than trying to find music work in general. You've still got to play as much as you can. Network as much as you can. You never know who you're going to meet on any given gig.

That particular gig may not be that great, but the drummer may happen to be the MD for your favorite artist. You never know. Also, be a nice person! Arrogance is a turn-off. Then there's plain old luck. Someone once told me that being a successful musician was 20% talent, 20% persistence and 60% luck.

(JC) How important is image with regard to getting and maintaining work in NYC as a sideman?

(MG) In the end, I think your talent and personality is what will get you gigs as a sideman, more often than not. I'm not sure that an "image" is vital, but it's not a bad idea to look good when you're working, no matter what your job is!

(JC) What can you suggest to bassists interested in breaking into the Broadway scene?

(MG) I started subbing on the Broadway production of *Movin' Out* from the beginning of the run. When they started putting together the first national tour, I made it known that I was interested in doing it. They also asked me to be the Band Director, which I said yes to.

Broadway is one of the last steady paychecks left for musicians in NYC. Because of this, there are now world class musicians playing in Broadway shows who you wouldn't have found there ten years ago. It's a very small circle of people and there is certainly no shortage of musicians.

I would suggest finding out who the bass player is on a show and getting in touch with him or her to see if they need a sub. It's a hard circle to crack, but you never know. If you get a shot, step up and learn the book backwards and forwards so the MD is impressed and hopefully you'll get asked back.

(JC) What kind of basses are you playing these days? Why have you chosen these instruments?

(MG) My main basses are a Sadowsky NYC four string and an older Tobias Signature five. I also have a 66 J bass, a 64 P bass, and a great MTD Fretless for when that sound is calling. The Sadowsky sounds and plays great no matter where I'm playing or what I'm playing it through. Roger's pre-amp is legendary with good reason, and I've never played a more true fretboard. The Tobias is an extension of myself. I bought it new when I was nineteen and continue to be astounded by how it sounds, how I connect with it and the creativity it brings out of me. What's left to say about vintage Fenders that hasn't been said? They stand the test of time and bring a certain kind of warmth and vibe that only an old Fender can.

www.MalcolmGold.com
www.MySpace.com/MalcolmGold

Bassist: Malcolm Gold
Interviewed by: John Carey

www.JohnCarey.net

Photo by Jos L Knaepen

Interview with Belgian/NYC bassist, Reggie Washington:

Reggie Washington is a bassist living in Brussels, Belgium, and New York City. He has worked with Lester Bowie, Branford Marsalis, World Saxophone Quartet, Mor Chiam, Mike Mainieri & Steps Ahead, Roy Hargrove, Will Smith, M-Base Collective, Ute Lemper, Uri Caine, Richard Leo Johnson, Omar Hakim, Steve Jordan, Onaje Allan-Gumbs, Cassandra Wilson, Jimmy Cobb, Keith Copeland, Kenny Washington, Mino Cinelu, Lenny White, Steve Coleman, Buddy Williams, Kenny Garrett, Marvin "Smitty" Smith, Pino Palladino, Baba Olantunji, Ravi Coltrane, Bernard Purdie, Jeff "Tain" Watts, Oliver Lake, Jimmy Lovelace, Dave Fiuczynski, Horacio "El Negro" Hernandez, Gene Lake, Billy Kilson, Dave Valentin, Dafnis Prieto, Anthony Hamilton, Keith Carlock, Ronnie Cuber, Anton Fig, Greg Osby, Mike Clark, Terri-Lyne Carrington, Mario Rivera, Frank McComb, Marcus Strickland, Cornelius Bumphus, Matthew Garrison, Dré Pallemaerts, Skoota Warner, Magic Malik, Dave Holland, Jef-Lee Johnson, Poogie Bell, Valerie Simpson, Archie Shepp, Marque Gilmore, Salif Keita, Stéphane Galland, Don Byron, David Gilmore, Cheick-Tidiane Seck, Meshell N'degeocello, Jean-Paul Bourelly, Kenny Kirkland, D'Angelo, Chico Hamilton, Arturo O'Farrill, Lester Bowie and Arthur Blythe, to name but a few.

In 1962, Reggie was born into a musical family, with parents who were avid music lovers and a brother and sister who influenced him tremendously as well. Reggie studied cello privately through school, playing in many orchestras. He performed with the New York Philharmonic Orchestra under conductors Zubin Mehta, James Levine and Claudio Abbado. In high school, he then switched to acoustic bass. Reggie studied upright bass classically with William Blossom. He studied jazz with Paul West, and studied Afro-Cuban music with Victor Venegas. Reggie decided to pick up the electric bass after spending many musical nights with his brother, Kenny Washington, and the great Marcus Miller.

(JC) Do you agree that jazz has a more appreciative audience in Europe these days in comparison to New York? Has it always been this way or is this shift in interest a recent one?

(RW) Some musicians from the States have made the move in the past based on love. I did. There are a lot of American musicians I know that now live in Europe: Jean-Paul Bourelly, Darryl Hall, Joe Bowie, Marque Gilmore, John Arnold, Kenny Martin, David Murray, Owen Hart Jr., Rasuul Saadiq and Sadiq Bey to name a few.

I also left NYC because of the sad state of the music scene. No real work. Club owners don't pay cats, so you basically play for the door. In some clubs the music is purely background ("Can you play a little softer? You sound great though!") . . . dinner from the musician's menu, one drink per set, get paid peanuts and leave. There's no respect. Europe has started copying the States, giving less respect to the music than before. Promoters are pinching pennies with booking new or rising acts. They're into booking names only to put butts in the seats! The "elite" American artists are booked over and over, year after year. Where's the variety? The big labels have a stronghold on festivals. They push their big name artists and push out independent labels with lesser known yet equally as talented artists.

There has always been a more appreciative audience in Europe, but this nonsense of no gigs is a *universal* thing! The industry is suffering. Multimedia and technology have made it easy to be a musician or recording artist. When we use to say to folks twenty to thirty years ago that you're recording an album, you were considered special. Now? Everybody does a demo in their own crib.

Hard work is not being recognized. If we speak about clubs (no large venues), in New York, tourists will pay twenty dollars plus a set and will not really think twice. In Europe, people pay less and think it's already expensive. Both the States and Europe have no clue of all the work we invest in the music!

(JC) If you could select five attributes (musically or personally) that a bassist must have in order to be a working bassist here in New York, what would they be?

(RW) There are *no* particular attributes that'll get you through the gauntlet of NYC! I've seen cats get chewed up and spit out! They were well prepared and had the right attitude. The intangibles can get you. A knucklehead boy or girlfriend or a bad diet can make you lose focus and all of a sudden . . . whoosh, the under current gets you. The greatest attribute is the ability to stay away from morons and assholes. Stay away from folks that drink and drug too much! That's the way to screw up everything. Doing drugs and drinking until you barf doesn't get you any closer to musical nirvana, just closer to rehab . . . or impending death! I stopped drinking and puffing last year. My playing has improved. I'm more focused and creative. I'm more in-tune with the business. You can't do that when you're drunk and high.

New York is too fast. It's a lesson and proving ground for the player willing to learn. You have to be open to everything, willing to listen and embrace. I've learned all over. From playing on the street (1982-85) to the late night clubs uptown with Greg Bandy and Jimmy Ponder, you can find all types of music to embrace there. These teachings I use to this day. That's the beauty of The Apple.

If you need to be something, you need to be yourself and you need to know what you want. You need to have a deed or a purpose. This is for everywhere.

(JC) Can you describe the music business when you were first entering the NYC music scene? Was there a sense of a "community of musicians?" What was it like getting work then?

(RW) The younger generation of musicians is spoiled. We now live in a more individual, "me" world. Before there was the Internet, there was more person-to-person contact! Now we're in a virtual world. The communication between musicians (face-to-face) is far less than in previous years. Cats came to your gig and acted as the "rooting section." Now musicians come to hate or look for ways to steal your gig!

A community? Dude! It was like "passing the torch" down with the older cats when I was coming up. The older guys I was around were in my ass to step up . . . *all* positive: "Learn those tunes young blood!" They'd make you stay on the bandstand to get it right. Being a bass player in that environment was a godsend! Having one of the baddest jazz drummers as a brother (Kenny) posed a unique problem, however; folks took it for granted that I knew every jazz tune. They would count off the tunes and say to me, "You're Kenny Washington's brother! I know you know this tune." Luckily I'd heard the tunes at home listening to records with my brother. Any given night you could play with . . . anybody! I was doing the jam session at the Village Gate about twenty years ago. All kinds of players came in to have a drink and play before their gig. We started at three pm and it ended at nine pm Saturdays and Sundays. That opportunity doesn't really exist anymore. Jam sessions are not learning experiences like they were before. It's become a hangout for wannabes and sad cats who want to pad their music bio (I played with. . .). Folks play the same tunes weekly and play the role. Eric Lewis, Ron Affif and Julius Tolentino are the only guys running "legit" jam sessions! When I was coming up, we came to the sessions to learn, play and to show ourselves on the scene. I remember meeting James Genus that way. He used to come to the Village Gate and sit-in. He was one of the only electric players to come and play. Of course I was very territorial with my gig. I vibed a little bit, but after that, we learned from each other and the other healthy competition. He's a great player and a good friend to this day.

In NYC, everything is happening. People are there now trying to get a piece of the pie. I'm a native New Yorker. I didn't get a gig under my name until *after* I left for Brussels! (Thank you Christian at The Blue Note.) Musicians come to NYC to play and are willing to play for nothing, just for the experience of playing on a New York stage. Some of these kids come to New York with *no* edge or desire! Mom and dad pay the rent. No worries. This has an effect on the entire fabric of the scene. Cats don't think twice about undercutting each other for a gig. No solidarity. The community or family vibe is gone or only in certain places. That's what made it so special.

(JC) When did you leave NYC to move to Brussels? How would you describe the state of the music business in NYC when you left concerning bass related work?

(RW) I left New York during a tour with Roy Hargrove & RH Factor in 2005. Before that I was thinking of relocating to Europe just to get a different perspective. On that tour (2003-05) the band was frequently in Europe pushing the CD, *Hard Groove*, on Verve. I was only home in the city long enough to get financial matters in order and then back out. The expression, "out of sight, out of mind" is a true and dangerous one in NYC! People hear about you on-tour and don't see you . . . you can be forgotten. During that time, the city gig situation was bleak for me. Between the little musician's niches and specialized music clubs, the closing of good clubs and non paying places along with people thinking they can't call you because you work with someone they view as elite, the scene was empty! I was doing the occasional club date gig with Manhattan Swing (thanks Joe!) and some hits with close friends. I thought, what's the use? No gigs . . . no respect . . . see ya!!!

At the same time The Most High brought Stefany (my honey/manager) into my life and she pushed me to become a leader. We've built something together that I couldn't have done in New York. (Thanks Stef!) Now, friends from New York that work with me in my band in Europe (Skoota Warner, Marcus & E.J. Strickland and David Gilmore) tell me the NYC scene is really suffering. It has become worse than when I was there. That's sad news.

(JC) You use Woody Phifer's basses. What do you like about them?

(RW) I've known Woody Phifer for twenty-five plus years. You and I spoke about this before. That's the relationship you need to have with someone if you intend to make music your life's work. I don't understand cats with eight to ten basses! If you can't play that one, how you gonna play the other nine? I always thought it was *you* who made the sound? I have one four string electric bass and my acoustic bass. I play *all* styles on my "Fanny Neck" bass.

The CD's from the last fifteen years (Steve Coleman, Branford Marsalis, Don Byron, Cassandra Wilson, etc.) were played on my "Queen Neck." Two years ago that neck was badly damaged and Woody made me the "Fanny Neck." The body has been the same Woody "Altered" body for sixteen years! Same hardware and electronics! Don't try to fix something that works. Woody's making me another bass in the coming year.

I've had a *total* of four basses in my life! Woody has been there through every one. He is, in my opinion, a genius. He's a guitar player as well as a gifted luthier and he understands the "eccentric ways" of the player. He has a complete knowledge of the instrument and is willing to drop knowledge on cats . . . if you're worthy and willing to listen. When he made my basses, I was there! We had conversations, discussions, arguments (he won) and brainstorms together to make the best instrument for me. He knows what I like in my bass. The feel, sound, look, everything: the frets, wood, weight and hardware. Even the number of coats of finish! All of this anal, painstaking work yields a unique, beautiful and killer sounding instrument. Forget endorsements. I have a relationship with Woody! Imagine going to your bass luthier and get work done on your bass, talk about life and have dinner. Good time all around! I love his personal touch. We work well together. That's what I need. I'll never play another instrument. Phifer Designs is it!!! (www.phiferdesigns.com)

(JC) How has recently having a beautiful baby girl changed you (musically and/or personally)?

(RW) I'm a dad for the third time. My oldest daughter Simone is fifteen, my son Reuben is nine and baby Ella is one and a half months. She brings meaning to everything again. It makes me want to have my kids all in one place! Having a child and being sober and clean of drugs and alcohol is the best feeling in the world. I cheated myself out of quality time with my kids, being mean and hung over the day after a gig or late night recording session.

Musically, the clean mind is so much more receptive. Music is flooding in for me to record at home. My playing is stronger now. I'm beginning to practice in front of her. Ella's an energy source! She (and Maman) pretty much keeps me on the ball. There are more on the horizon. (Three more???)

www.MySpace.com/ReggieWashington
www.JamminColors.com

Bassist: Reggie Washington
Interviewed by: John Carey

www.JohnCarey.net

Photo by Jonas Bostrom

Interview with NYC bassist, Janek Gwizdala:

Janek Gwizdala is a professional bassist, producer and music director in New York City. He currently is the MD and bass player for ATO/RCA recording artist JEM and bass player for jazz guitarist, Mike Stern. Born in England, Janek moved to NYC in 2000. His credits include work with Mike Stern, Randy Brecker, Airto Moirera, Pat Metheny, Flora Purim, Bob Malach, Hiram Bullock, Paul Shaffer, Kenwood Dennard, Marcus Miller, Wayne Krantz, Bob James, Billy Cobham, John Patitucci, Eric Johnson, Bob Mintzer, Ronny Jordan, Terri Lyne Carrington, Jojo Mayer, Gary Husband, Mark Turner, Arturo Sandoval, Danny Gottlieb, Peter Cincotti, Rick Margitza, Tony Royster Jr, Richie Morales, Scott Kinsey, Gregoire Maret, Lew Solof, Andy Milne, Jive Jones, Mike Phillips, JEM, John Ellis, NERVE, Dapp Theory, Aaron Goldberg, Jeff Lorber, Wayman Tisdale, Oz Noy, Lionel Loueke, Jose Neto, Najee, Frank McComb, Billy Pierce, Paul Oakenfold, Cafe, Stevie Winwood, Barry Altschul, Buddy Williams, Torsten De Winkel, Liquid Todd, Adam Freeland, Randy Bernsen and Domonique Di Piazza.

His own CD release, *Live at the 55 Bar*, features Elliot Mason (trombone), Brad Mason (trumpet), Justin Vasquez (alto), Tim Miller (guitar), Oli Rockberger (keys) and Tobias Ralph (drums).

(JC) When did you come to New York City to pursue music, and what inspired you to make the move? How would you describe your initial impressions of the music scene when you first arrived?

(JG) Well I moved here in the summer of 2000 having spent three semesters at Berklee in Boston and then quit. I think I was inspired to make the move because of a few things: Berklee, or just being in school, wasn't where I wanted to be, and all of my heroes of the music I loved to play were living and playing in NYC. I was coming down here as much as I could while I was in school to hang out, and I just decided it would make more sense to be living here and to be a part of the scene rather than just being a visitor. Being twenty years old when I arrived, I really had no idea of the scene, but soon found out that you have to pay some serious dues before you're accepted into it. I had already done a bunch of nice gigs but it seemed to be a completely new thing when I moved here. I had very few gigs and spent most of my first year here just hanging out and shedding.

(JC) How have you seen the music business change with regard to bass related work since you first arrived?

(JG) Well a year after I got here 9/11 happened which changed the face of the music scene for everyone, not just bass players. Clubs closed, people didn't go out to hang as much, and some cats I knew moved away even. It was a long time before things started getting back to their bustling self after that. I know that I spent a lot of time on the road when I was first living in NYC, mainly doing tours in Europe and some stuff on the West coast as there wasn't a lot going on in the city. I also realized that no one wanted to play jazz with an electric bass player, and what few gigs there were for electric bass players in an improvised setting were taken by players like Matt Garrison with Herbie, Richard Bona with Zawinul, and at the time players like Lincoln Goines, Anthony Jackson, etc. with Mike Stern.

So I got myself a Mac and a cracked copy of Logic and started teaching myself about the technology side of the industry. I got into songwriting, programming and production in a big way. I was also fortunate enough to play on a couple of randomly big record dates which kept me going money wise for a while before I was asked to produce a fairly heavy record date for a guitarist by the name of Ronny Jordan. That was my first break in production, and although I totally got screwed on the business end of things, it did lead to a lot of other work and taught me a lot about that side of the scene in NYC.

(JC) In what capacity have you worked with Mike Stern, and what is it like working with him?

(JG) Well I am one of about six bass players that plays with Mike on a semi regular basis. We were introduced by a friend of mine in the UK who had been at Berklee with Mike in the 70s. We played phone tag for many years, running into each other at the 55 Bar saying that we must play together at some point. Then a couple of years ago we got together at his place, started playing and immediately hit it off. We've been really good friends ever since and have worked together a bunch. I've been on the road with him in the US and abroad; we've done some stuff in the studio together, did a short DVD recording, and more important than anything for me, we shed together all the time. I'll go over to his place and we'll just play for hours on end. We both have crazy busy schedules so we don't do it as much as I would like, but when we do it's priceless. He was one of the first people I ever transcribed and checked out when I was getting into jazz, so it's great to be a part of this scene.

(JC) What attributes (musically or personally) must a bass player have to be a working player here in New York City?

(JG) Be mentally very strong because this is the hardest city in the world to work in. One minute everything is cool, and the next minute everything can be the total opposite. Like in any city or scene, you have to be cool to hang out with. Everyone wants it to be easy when they work with you, and you'll get many more calls and recommendations by being easy to work with.

I'm not sure I have much more to say about what to do to work in New York besides that. I have lived here for eight years, but never really aspired to just work here. My scene has been on the road. So much so that I never really built up enough of a reputation for being an "in town" cat to call for certain gigs. If you go out of town for any reason, don't tell anyone. As soon as you go away for a weekend gig and start telling people, they will think you're gone for a month. I hear people leaving the classic, "I'm going to be out of town until the blah of blah . . ." Never do that. You're in town, period. Have a cell phone that works wherever you are, and always just get back to people.

I've just never really been that "in town" person. In fact it's only in the past six months that I've been working regularly with my own group promoting this new album. I think because of that I've been getting more calls to play on other people's projects in town. I have basically been living at the 55 Bar playing up to ten gigs a month there sometimes.

(JC) Can you discuss your new CD release, *Live at the 55 Bar*? Where is it available for purchase, who is playing on it and what were your inspirations for the making of it?

(JG) The new album was written specifically for the players I hired for the date. It is groove based music with some of the greatest soloists the New York jazz scene has to offer. The main concept for the album was groove and melody. I wanted to write some very simple harmonic and melodic music that any listener from any walk of life could come and listen to and take something away with them. It's been a real blast having this album out for the past few months, and great fun playing every month at the 55 Bar with this incredible group of musicians.

We've also had some special guests with the band that have included Randy Brecker, Gregoire Maret, Zach Danziger and Bob Reynolds. I'm working on releasing some tracks from those shows, all of which we've recorded. I'm about to start a two year world tour as musical director with the singer/songwriter Jem, so I'm planning dates with my band on the road to coincide with breaks from the pop tour. You can pick up the album at www.janekgwizdala.com and keep your eyes on the Myspace page at www.myspace.com/janekgwizdalaproject for all tour dates and information of new releases.

www.JanekGwizdala.com
www.MySpace.com/JanekGwizdalaProject

Bassist: Janek Gwizdala
Interviewed by: John Carey

www.JohnCarey.net

Interview with NYC bassist, Ivan "Funkboy" Bodley:

Ivan "Funkboy" Bodley is a bass player and music director to many well-known bands and artists. He has performed with nineteen Rock and Roll Hall of Fame inductees and counting. Ivan is currently the music director with Sam Moore (of Sam & Dave), Martha Reeves and the Vandellas, The Shirelles, The Crystals, The Tokens and has performed with artists like Sting, Wynonna Judd, Travis Tritt, David Foster, The Uptown Horns, Peter Wolf, Solomon Burke, Bo Diddley, Gloria Gaynor, Buster Poindexter, Percy Sledge, and Rufus and Carla Thomas, to name a few. Ivan recently produced, arranged and recorded his second CD, "iBOD," (available at: www.cdbaby.com/cd/ivanbodley2) in the Funklab, his studio in Brooklyn, NY. The record includes musicians Gil Parris (guitar), Ben Stivers (keyboard) and Ronny Drayton (guitar).

(JC) How has your education assisted in your "real life" musical endeavors as a working bassist, music director and sideman? Do you think having a formal education in music is mandatory in order to be a successful player here in NYC?

(IB) Berklee filled in a lot of gaps in my knowledge and ability. I had been playing semi-pro for about ten years before I went to Berklee. So a lot of it was putting "names to faces," so to speak. Once the foundation was filled in, the school really helped me build on that.

(JC) How long have you been a bassist in New York? What were your initial impressions of the music scene when you first arrived?

(IB) I've been in NYC fifteen years now. It's been great. I've lived in Chattanooga, New Orleans, Los Angeles, London and Boston. But for me, the music and players I identify with most come from New York City.

(JC) How has the music scene changed since you have been here in New York, with regard to getting work as a sideman?

(IB) When I first got to town I heard a lot of talk that the studio scene and jingle business of the 70s and 80s had dried up. It had. But rather than crying over spilled milk, it was time to figure out the next paradigm for making a living in music.

And now I feel like the "live" club scene in NYC from the 90s has dried up thanks to our last two draconian elitist mayors. So what do we do now, leave? It's time to constantly reinvent. There are always opportunities out there, especially in a city this cosmopolitan, even though the old ways of doing business no longer necessarily apply.

(JC) What advice can you give to those bassists who are already competent bassists here in New York, but are seeking work with higher profile artists?

(IB) That's a tough one in a way. I've heard the same thing for years about how to do it. It's all time and dedication and persistence. My stuff has been all word of mouth. So you can imagine that these contacts are made very slowly, very deliberately, and over a long period of time.

But I will say this . . . Play as much as possible with as many people as possible. Even though your goal may be Madison Square Garden, taking a $30 blues gig in an Irish bar might eventually get you that gig (at MSG). And never think that any gig is "beneath" you. I can't tell you how many friends of mine have gotten off of huge world tours to be happily back on Bleecker Street the next day.

Your question already assumes that the players are competent, but you have to strive for excellence in all things: playing in tune, playing in time, being on time, being in uniform, having a positive attitude, having a website, having and actively distributing business cards, having a car, a tux, having gear that works, etc.

(JC) If you had to choose only five attributes (musically or personally) that a bassist must have in order to survive as a working bassist in NYC, what would they be?

(IB)

1. Congeniality. Be a nice person. With two musicians of equal ability, the nicer cat is going to get the gig.

2. Consistency. Play your ass off at all times, no matter where, no matter what material. You never know who's listening. Treat every gig as if it were Madison Square Garden.

3. Reliability. Answer all of your calls and emails immediately. Show up on time. Don't make people who hire you have to chase you or check up on you.

4. Taste. Know the music that you're playing as intimately as possible, and especially know and understand what your roll is within that music. Jaco licks seldom work on a Zydeco gig. Slapping on a country gig is generally a stretch. And you'll probably want to leave your upright at home should Ozzy call you.

5. Honesty. Deal with people the way you want them to deal with you. Too often the dog-eat-dog aspect of the music business makes it seem like we're just waiting to break off a piece for ourselves, all others be damned when it's our turn. But it's a collective haul no matter what level of the business. Even if I

occasionally get ripped off by unscrupulous individuals, I sleep better at night knowing that I've dealt with people fairly.

www.Funkboy.net
www.MySpace.com/FunkBoyNYC

Bassist: Ivan "Funkboy" Bodley
Interviewed by: John Carey

www.JohnCarey.net

Interview with NYC bassist, Li'nard:

Li'nard is a New York City bass player and versatile singer, songwriter and producer. Li'nard plays many genres of music including dance, funk, Hip Hop and R&B, West African, rock, blues and reggae. Li'nard has worked with Patti LaBelle, The O'Jays and The Jones Girls, and he has contributed to over fifty albums. Before moving to New York, Li'nard played up and down the Eastern seaboard and toured Europe with the groups Defunkt, Mr. Thing and the Professional Human Beings. Li'nard has also performed with Codaryl Moffett Jazz Ensemble and Roy Ayers. He heads his band, Li'nard's Many Moods, which can be seen weekly at Club Groove, NYC.

(JC) You often sings lead vocals while playing bass. How did you go about working on singing and playing bass at the same time?

(L) I started out singing in the choir at the church I attended at four years old, so singing has always felt like a natural thing to do, not something I would think about; it is like a natural reaction. So when I started playing the bass, and came to the point where I was going to do gigs, it was just natural to sing and play at the same time. Some songs are harder to play and sing than others. There are some songs where the rhythm of the bass line is so different from the vocal line that I can't sing at all on those types of songs. That doesn't happen too often, but there are some songs that are like that. For the person trying to work on this, I suggest that you either learn the bass line first, or the words that you are going to sing first. This way you don't have to focus on learning both at the same time. Then you can focus your concentration on one or the other, and do the other naturally.

(JC) How long have you been working as a bassist in NYC? What were your initial impressions when you first arrived to New York, with regard to the music scene?

(L) I have been working on the New York Music Scene since 1990. I stopped for a while to take care of some things, but got back on the scene in 1993. My impression of the New York Scene was just like any other scene around the world. There were a lot of musician trying to get the same work, and they approached things in a competitive type of way, instead of what music is suppose to be about (being creative and giving). So for me, it's not a healthy environment because it sparks musicians to sometime treat each other in not so pleasant of ways.

(JC) How has the music scene changed over the years you've been here, specifically in relation to getting work as a bassist/sideman?

(L) As for the music scene, it has changed drastically. There are not a lot of clubs that support the art anymore. It is harder to find club owners that will pay decent money for a night of entertainment. The election of Mayor Giuliani and Mayor Bloomberg has killed the music industry in New York City.

(JC) How long have you been a "main stay" at Club Groove, NYC, and can you share some of your most memorable experiences there?

(L) I have been working at the Groove now for over seven years. For me, the most memorable times always are when people come from all over the world and tell me that they organized the entire vacation to come see me play at the Groove. It is such an incredible feeling to have someone come up and say that. I have heard it quite a bit, but it is always amazing that people do that. That leaves a lasting impression on me. Also, like you said, the crowd at the Groove is always entertaining. At one point when we first started playing the Groove, we were getting women showing off their breasts every weekend. That was pretty interesting. We were not encouraging this, but it seemed like the word was getting around, and each week there would be two or three women showing there breasts like it was a competition or something. That was definitely one of the most memorable experiences at the club!

(JC) If you had to choose only five attributes (musically or personally) a bassist must have in order to be a working bassist in NYC, what would they be?

(L) The five attributes I would suggest are:
1. Know yourself.
2. Believe in yourself.
3. Stay focused on your own agenda.
4. Fix a plan just for yourself.
5. Have trust in what you are doing.

www.Li-nardsManyMoods.com

Bassist: Li'nard
Interviewed by: John Carey

www.JohnCarey.net

Interview with NYC bassist, Paul Frazier:

Paul Frazier is a professional bassist, singer, writer, producer, studio and indie record label owner in New York City. He is currently bassist for David Byrne with whom he has worked for over seven years. Paul is also currently playing with the brand new original trio, Farm League Funk. He has worked with Lucy Woodward, Kirsten Price, Jason Blum and The Take Out Kings, The Mark Pender Band, Amel Larrieux, Lev's Boom Box, Amanda Homi, Shoshana Bean, The Spinnoza's, Justin Mathew, Emily Zuzik, Nadia Ackerman and Astroglide. In the past, Paul has worked with many artists and producers such as The Funky Poets (as co-leader of 90s Sony group), Arrested Development, Forro in the Dark, Norah Jones, Scissor Sisters, Damien Rice, Michael Tolcher, Pop Rocks, Ultra Blue (featuring Dave Stryker, Dave Mann, Rachel Z, Pete Belasco, and Kevin Mahogany), Imani Coppola, Shawn Colvin, Mic Murphy, David Frank, Chaka Khan, Pat Ciscarano, The Weather Girls, Joss Stone, Mike Mangini, Cab and Chris Calloway and Donny Osmond to name but a few.

Paul received gold and platinum honors for writing and producing music in the movie *Free Willy*. He has appeared on and scored vocal arrangements when with the Funky Poets on the HBO series *Oz*, *Della Ventura* (CBS weekly drama) and *Firehouse* (a CBS Fontana-Levinson production featuring Richard Dean Anderson).

(JC) How long have you been involved in the New York City music scene, and how have you seen it change over the years, with regard to bass related work?

(PF) Since the early 80s, I've been here in the live and studio scene. There was a lot of bass synth playing going on, but there was also plenty of groovin' players at that time. I think when sampling came in, bass players were losing out on sessions because the samples were proven bass lines from the past; so how could you compete against the already recognizable lines?

Over the past ten or so years, bass players have been getting work, but the budgets for tours and sessions aren't the same as the big record company days (although there are some artists who still can pay well). I remember when there was a small circle of bass players who seemed to be on all the sessions in NYC. But now with all the home studios, there are a lot of bass players whose work is out there. The landmark clubs where artists would build a following are quickly disappearing and are being replaced by condos and drug store chains. There are some new places that are cool and a few of the established places are still left.

(JC) If you had to choose five attributes (musically or personally) that a bass player must have in order to be a working bassist here in New York, what would they be?

(PF)
1. Listen to a lot of styles and understand the feels of each, because laying into a groove on any kind of music is very important.

2. Reading music will help and so will your ears. Listen to others and not just yourself.

3. Get to know your fellow musicians because no one is going to call or recommend someone they don't know.

4. Eight out of ten times, less is more!!!

5. Don't be a jerk.

(JC) What advice can you give to those bassists who are already very competent bassists in NYC, but are seeking work with higher profile artists?

(PF) Although some of it was being in the right place at the right time, just knowing so many people here in NYC and trying to make sure that I do my job and then some will hopefully leave a good impression. So when the high profile gig comes along, your name gets thrown in the pot. The NYC bass brunch is a great way for young and/or out of town players to meet some of the guys who have been playing with high profile artists.

(JC) How important is developing one's "image" for bassists and sidemen in general? And what other business oriented (non-musical) tips might you give players?

(PF) I would say that developing your image doesn't hurt. An artist's manager and label always wants a musician to look the part, but if you're a nice enough guy and maybe wash every now and then, that helps too! Understand how the music business has changed and adjust to it. Get your music and playing up on a website. Network ... Go see good music where there will be musicians and producers hanging out where you can meet them. That leaves the arena gigs and dance clubs with $30 covers out!

(JC) What are your main basses for live and recording purposes? Have you been playing these instruments all along, or have you tried many in order to find what you truly enjoy?

(PF) I've always loved my old Fender Jazz with flatwounds. I also use a Bossa OB-5. This is a pretty versatile bass and has been good to me over the years. I also use a Rob Allen fretless five string which is great! It has such a warm sound with the nylon strings and it keeps getting better. I've been playing these basses for a while but as a lefty, I'm still searching for the perfect fretted bass. Jimmy Coppola makes a great bass, so I might get one of those before my next tour. You just can't walk in a store and find something to play when you're lefty.

www.MySpace.com/Paul_Frazier

Bassist: Paul Frazier
Interviewed by: John Carey

www.JohnCarey.net

Photo by John Carey

Interview with NYC bassist, Frank Gravis:

Frank Gravis is a professional bassist located in NYC since 1977. He has played and/or toured with Herbie Mann, David Sanborn, Hiram Bullock, Jack McDuff, Suzanne Vega, Rupert Holmes, Donna Summer, Dr. John, Otis Rush, Paul Butterfield, Bo Diddley, Jorge Dalto, Zhané, Toninho Horta, Ray Barretto, Cy Coleman, Angelo Badalamenti and many others. He has also played on countless television and radio commercials. Frank provided the bass line for the 1979 #1 hit, *Escape* (The Pina Colada song), by Rupert Holmes. He continues to play in and around New York, as well as teaching bass at The Collective.

(JC) What would you say most new cats on the scene need, with regard to skill, in order to get consistent work here?

(FG) I got here in 1977, so the scene back then is much different than it is now. Back in that era, there was a lot more work being done by live bassists. Since there was no MIDI and no computers, there was a whole lot more recording work as well as live gigs. Nowadays, those gigs are much fewer. So if a young bassist is going to come here to get work, he needs several important skills: reading, the ability to groove, knowledge of all different genres that require bass, and social skills are of paramount importance.

(JC) What is the most common weakness that you come across in students these days?

(FG) I have found that the one thing the students lack in common is the ability to really lock in and groove in a rhythm section, to the point of being able to take control and lead the band alongside the drummer to provide the groove that the music requires.

(JC) Other than your obvious knowledge of the instrument and skill level, to what do you attribute your own ability to maintain steady bass work in New York City since the 1970s?

(FG) My survival has completely depended on my ability to remake myself and learn new genre. When recording work became scarce, I learned the repertoire to do single engagements, which led to doing high-society club dates, which is the New York moniker for society gigs. That music is drawn from the standard American song repertoire. I have been doing that work since the late 80s, and I continue to do quite a bit of it today. I have also played in a Dominican Merengue band, a country-western band, a Latin-jazz group, several rock n roll bands and several R&B bands, to name a few. I still get called to play all these genres frequently. Having played in groups that play these types of music has enhanced me as a musician.

(JC) If you could pick five essential attributes (musically or personally) that a bass player needs to be both a good player and to remain on the scene, what would they be?

(FG) Reading, the ability to create a groove with a drummer, being prepared for the gig, having the right gear for whatever gig comes your way and being an easy person to get along with.

(JC) Are you still using the ESP 400 series basses as your main axes, and if so, what attracts you to them? I understand that the

craftsmanship that the ESP shop in Japan produces some of the best work in the world. Can you discuss what you like about these basses?

(FG) At the time I got these [ESP] instruments, which was the mid 80s, the quality of Fender's basses was getting really bad. That has changed somewhat, in that Fender has started paying attention to quality again. Their new American Standard basses are actually pretty good. However, they're still no match; the ESP 400 series basses from the 80s are still for my money way better. Since that time, guys like Roger Sadowsky and Jimmy Coppolo have started making truly great basses. In spite of that, I am sticking with my beloved ESP Jazz bass clones.

www.MySpace.com/FrankGravis

Bassist: Frank Gravis
Interviewed by: John Carey

www.JohnCarey.net

Interview with L.I./NYC bassist, Roy De Jesus:

Roy De Jesus is a professional bassist and bass educator located in New York. He studied bass guitar at B.I.T. in California, and he later opened his own school for electric bass in New York (Center for Learning). Roy uses four and five string fretted and fretless electric basses, and he plays all genres of music including jazz, fusion, funk, blues and rock. Roy has recorded/performed with The Upper Room Music Company, Paula Atherton, Clyde Jones, Liquid Children, Willie Steele, Mark Miller, Frank Vignola, Crissy Lawless, Steve Briody, Melanie Dekker, Matthew Villaflor, Ramona Machson, Michael Visconti, the Central Park Orchestra and many more artists and bands.

(JC) You have focused on playing all genres of music convincingly, as opposed to specializing within one specific genre. What was your reasoning behind this?

(RD) I have always been exposed to a lot of different styles of music, and looking back, I think listening is really a big part of it all. I'm Puerto Rican so we had Salsa being played in the house along with a blend of disco, jazz, funk and rock. In the 70s, you had so much new music being introduced on a daily basis. I would put the radio on and just try to listen and imitate what they were doing. My Mom was really into music and she was a big influence. I still remember her buying the Brothers Johnson's first album and telling me, "You have to check this out, they're really great . . ." (and I wasn't even playing bass yet). Just being around it really helped me once I started working. So I really didn't have a goal; I had an early love and passion for music so it just came naturally. I have tried to teach my students to be well-rounded musicians and to be familiar with all styles of music, especially if you want to be a working musician.

(JC) You are one of several bassists that in addition to making music, you've decided to get a day job in order to make a living. Can you discuss why you went this route?

(RD) My family was growing and although I was making a good living as a musician, it still wasn't enough to get by. At the time, I had just gotten into using computers for writing and recording music, and I ended up getting a job in that field. Now I am able to concentrate on my playing.

(JC) How have you seen the music business change over the past twenty to thirty years, and how has it affected you as a working bassist?

(RD) It seems to me that there are less and less places available for live music. I do a lot of club dates in NYC, and over the years DJ's have taken a lot of work away from the working musician. For example, years ago, one particular location might have had four rooms with a band in each room . . . they now have all DJ's instead. You do actually have some DJ companies incorporating live musicians, however. I have also done some TV work but some shows prefer to not have live music. With the advent of computers, iPods, the Internet, YouTube, etc., it seems like it's easy to just have music available to everyone whenever you want it. We are in the digital age. I'm actually working half as much but I'm making much more than I used to (with my particular band).

Another thing I see is that you just don't have a lot of young kids these days trying to perfect their craft. It's funny but it's getting to the point where people are going to say, "They're a live band and they actually play real instruments." With recording, I think you can get a lot of studio work but it tends to be smaller scale like demo work or self produced music.

(JC) If you had to choose only five attributes (musically or personally) that a bassist must have in order to be a working bassist in New York, what would they be?

(RD)
1. Listening.
2. Time and feel.
3. Discipline and hard work.
4. Keep challenging yourself.
5. Have an open personality.

AND ... have a good time, if you're enjoying yourself it shows.

(JC) Who are some of your favorite musicians (not just bassists)? What type of musicians do you enjoy working with and why?

(RD) I enjoy anything that grooves. Some of my favorite bands and players are The Beatles and their solo careers, Jaco Pastorius, Stanley Clarke, John Paul Jones, Larry Graham, Marcus Miller, Will Lee, Charlie Parker, Miles Davis, Anthony Jackson, Jimi Hendrix and John McLaughlin to mention a few. I love working with musicians that have a good musical "sense." Of course time and feel is important but just as important is knowing what to play and when to play it.

www.MySpace.com/RoyDeJesusMusic

Bassist: Roy De Jesus
Interviewed by: John Carey

www.JohnCarey.net

Interview with NYC bassist, Jeff Allen:

Originally from New Jersey, **Jeff Allen** is a professional electric and upright bassist and producer in New York City. He has both his bachelors and masters degrees from Juilliard in Classical String Bass. He has worked with Rosanne Cash, Marc Cohn, Duncan Sheik, Joan Osborne, Five For Fighting, The BoDeans, Stewart Copeland, David Sancious, Donna Lewis, Edie Brickel, Chantal Kreviazuk, Billy Preston, Toby Lightman, Chris Botti and Avril Lavigne, to name a few.

(JC) How old were you when you entered the NYC music scene? Can you describe your initial impressions when you first began working? What kind of work were you getting and how did you get it?

(JA) I was twenty-one or twenty-two. I graduated from school and pretty much straight away started playing in many different projects, most of which I got by responding to ads in the back of the Village Voice and going to auditions. The scene in New York at that time, the early 1990s, was incredibly healthy and vibrant. I had the great fortune to play in all sorts of groups, from R&B and rock bands to new music ensembles and hippie jam bands. Needless to say, the experience of both auditioning for and performing in so many diverse situations was an invaluable part of my education. Having to show up and be whoever you needed to be in any given situation truly helped me hone both my musical and personal skills.

(JC) This is a two part question: Do you feel it necessary to have a formal education in order to be a successful bassist working in NYC?

And what advice can you give to others who are already competent bassists in New York, but are seeking work with higher profile artists?

(JA) Answering the second question first, I think it primarily takes patience and perseverance to both establish a reputation that brings better work and build a wide enough client base of local artists, because you never know whose career will become what. As to having a formal education, I can definitely see both sides of that argument. Obviously, it's great to know what you're doing, but a formal education is not the only way to get to that point. While I don't think that the ability to read music is crucial to being an excellent and creative bass player, it does certainly open up additional avenues of work that might not otherwise be available.

(JC) Like several of the bassists I've interviewed, you are a "doubler," playing both electric and upright bass exceptionally well. Is there any disadvantage to playing both instruments? What benefits come from being able to play both?

(JA) The only disadvantage is that when people know you play both, they often want you to bring both— which, needless to say, can be bad for your back. Other than that, you're of course able to take a wider range of work. And, it can be quite cool the way certain stylistic elements on one instrument can cross-pollinate to the other. That said, I think of them as very different instruments in general, in both the physical demands they require and the choices they inherently force you to make stylistically. But overall, I like having the array of different voices to bring to the table.

(JC) How have you seen the music scene change over the years that you've been working in NYC? How has it affected you as a bassist?

(JA) Not to get too philosophical on your ass, but everything is constantly changing and nothing really remains the same. So yes, the scene continues to change, but that's beside the point. The question I think more about is how we need to adapt ourselves to an ever-evolving world, in terms of both diversifying our skill sets and expanding our notion of what our work should be.

(JC) If you had to choose five attributes (musically or personally) that a bassist must have to be a busy bassist in NYC, what would they be?

(JA)
1. Be able to connect with others without being an overly self-promoting douche.
2. Play well.
3. Preparation, preparation, preparation (H).
4. Gotta eat a breakfast.
5. Know about stuff other than music.

www.MySpace.com/JeffDAllen

Bassist: Jeff Allen
Interviewed by: John Carey

www.JohnCarey.net

Interview with L.I./NYC bassist, Kim Clarke:

Kim Clarke is a professional bassist, producer and educator and a veteran in the NYC music scene. She plays acoustic bass, electric upright and four and five-stringed electric bass guitars, as each situation demands. Kim earned a BA in Communications and Music from City College and Long Island University respectively, and is a three time recipient of the coveted N E A Jazz Study Fellowship. She has recorded twenty records with the famous avant-jazz funk band, Defunkt, a band where her bass playing has inspired bassists from all over the world (perhaps most notably is bassist, Flea, from the Red Hot Chili Peppers). In addition, Ms. Clarke has worked with George Gruntz, Annie Whitehead, Christy Doran, Marilyn Mazur, Ursula Dudziak, the National Black Theatre, Yusef Lateef Quartet, Teri Thornton Trio, Bertha Hope Trio, Robert Palmer, Kit McClure Big Band, Rachel Z Trio, Bigfood, Wallace Roney and Cindy Blackman Quartet, Oliver Lake and Jump Up, James Blood Ulmer Experience, Jack Mc Duff Quartet, Joe Henderson Quartet, Rodney Kendricks Quartet, Harold Ousley, Jimmy Heath, Steve Coleman, Lester Bowie, Andy Bey, Louis Hayes, Gerald Hayes, the late Lionel Hampton, Candido, Patato, Little Jimmy Scott, Dr. Billy Taylor, Olu Dara, Screamin Jay Hawkins, Dakota Staton, Gracian Moncur, the late Art Blakey, Philly Joe Jones, Marylou Williams, Sharon Freeman, Sheila Jordan, Geri Allen,

Vanessa Rubin, Cassandra Wilson, Fievre Latina, Adela Dalto, poets Ntozake Shange and Trazana Beverly, dancers Tina Pratt and Roxanne Butterfly, MAGNETS! and rapper/actress Queen Latifah.

Kim was influenced by her jazz loving father, her grandfather, Henry HY Clarke (trombonist and leader of the Alabamians), her blues loving mother and her son. In addition, she is influenced by Jimi Hendrix, bassist Johnny "Sean" Solomon (the first local black electric bassist to break into the rock scene) and many others. Ms. Clarke has been written about in the *Who's Who in the Performing Arts*, *Bass Player Magazine*, *Guitar Player Magazine*, Germany's *Jazzdimensions Online Magazine*, as well as a number of European magazines and several books on women in jazz. She is endorsed by Acoustic Image, ESP Guitars and Fight Sound, LLC.

(JC) When did you first enter the New York City music scene as a working bassist? What were your initial impressions at the time, and what were some of the first gigs you picked up?

(KC) After having learned a number of popular jazz standards on the bandstand at Kenny Gates Music Factory in Brooklyn, I entered the "scene." I stumbled upon Kenny Gates Music Factory by chance, and it changed my whole life. There were quite a few scenes in NY. The first for me was with a basement R&B band turn touring entity, Business Before Pleasure. The first theatrical gig for me was with the National Black Theatre in Harlem and my first Manhattan based jam sessions were at Art Blakey Junior's studio, Studio We, Studio Rivbee and The Ladies Fort. My first touring Jazz gig was with Brother Yusef Lateef.

(JC) How have you witnessed the scene here in NYC change over the years? What advice can you give to those considering moving to New York to pursue a career as bassist?

(KC) New York has changed a great deal. I have seen various clubs and workshops, people and mentors come and go. That is the nature of change. I think each individual's experience will be different according to who they are, what they want, what the particular musical elements are asking of them, how well they interact with the art and artists they work with, and how well they adjust to themselves as a channel of creativity or singular identity. Focusing on flexibility and fearlessness helps, but it is more important to respect the elders and the "pecking order." It also doesn't hurt to be able to read music well.

(JC) What do you believe is essential with regard to one's musicianship, personality and politics, when aspiring to be a full time bassist and "maintaining" one's career in music here in NYC?

(KC) One should study technique, relaxation, open-mindedness and empathy. Music has spiritual value and someone had to sweat or endure pain to create it. Respect it.

(JC) Can you discuss some of the advantages and disadvantages of playing both electric and acoustic bass? Is it challenging to maintain adequacy on both instruments?

(KC) The advantages are that you increase the opportunity to work and also have differing vehicles of expression. It is a challenge to maintain both, especially since life usually isn't a music camp and reality tries hard to take you somewhere else. It is good to be happy wherever you are with the knowledge that you can improve if you try.

(JC) Can you discuss the necessity of playing multiple genres of music in order to be a working bassist in NYC?

(KC) New York is a melting pot, more so than any other area. I've played with East Indian mandolinists that are into Hendrix, South Africans into bebop music, Native Americans and Cameroonians into the blues, Japanese swing dancers, avant-garde Korean Kimongo players, as well as strong Salsa elements of Tito Puente, Patato, Mario Rivera, etc. That's why NY is so dangerous: you can't hide the truth; it's your next door neighbor.

www.MySpace.com/KimClarkeOnBass

Bassist: Kim Clarke
Interviewed by: John Carey

www.JohnCarey.net

Interview with NYC bassist, Percy Jones:

Percy Jones is a bassist residing in New York City. He is perhaps the most revered fretless player alive, and he's inspired us all with his unique approach to the instrument. Percy has worked with Brian Eno, Elliott Sharp, Suzanne Vega, Brand X and TUNNELS, to name but a few. He is also a bass instructor and can be seen on the instructional video, *Bass Exploration of Percy Jones*.

(JC) When did you first move to New York City to pursue working as a bassist? How would you describe the music scene at this time, specifically with regard to getting work as a bassist?

(PJ) I moved to NYC in 1979 from London, England. At the time I didn't know too much about the NYC music scene; I had been playing in Brand X up to that point and my experience of this country was just based on doing tours. Soon after moving here things rapidly fell apart. Brand X got dumped by its management and record company, and I was without a gig. I got a job in Brooklyn moving furniture and continued to try and find a point of reference in my music life. One evening I was buying carrots in a supermarket in Park Slope when the drummer of Noise R Us walked up and invited me to a rehearsal. I ended up joining the band and started to meet more musicians on the NYC scene. Years later, after buying carrots in a store in Spanish Harlem I was duffed up and robbed by a gang. (This ended any notion I had that buying carrots brings good luck.) The thing I learned from all of this is that life is very unpredictable and you never know who you might run into at any time. I played with Noise R Us (later Paranoise) for quite some time and still record with guitarist Jim Matus on projects to this day.

So never get complacent about any success you might have. On the other hand, when things are bad, you never know what lies around the corner.

The NYC music scene at the time was pretty interesting. There was a fairly thriving jazz scene going on, and the punk thing was in full swing. The downtown scene was just beginning. The old Knitting Factory on Houston Street would open soon afterwards and that was one of the important venues for anyone trying to do new music. CBGB was there and Hilly Crystal would always give you a gig. I played there with Noise R Us, Tunnels, and I did a few solo gigs in there too; of course CBGB had a thriving NYC punk thing going on too, with the likes of the Ramones, etc.

(JC) How has the music scene changed in NYC since you have been working and living here? To what do you attribute any change? And how do you imagine the scene will continue to change over the next several years?

(PJ) The scene has changed quite a bit and not really for the better unfortunately. NYC is safer and cleaner than it's probably ever been, but the rising rents have forced a lot of good clubs to close. CBGB and The Bottom Line are just two examples. There are new small places springing up, many in Brooklyn interestingly enough, that put on interesting bands trying to break new ground. But there does seem to be a ton of bands playing around that are frankly not very original or interesting. I think it's one of the negative effects of gentrification in NYC. The jazz scene seems to now be mainly in the upper scale clubs like The Blue Note or Iridium which a lot of people simply cannot afford to go to. Things never stay the same so I'm hoping the local scene swings back to a more cutting edge thing.

(JC) What advice might you give to those bass players considering moving to NYC from overseas or out of state to pursue their musical endeavors? What might they need to be prepared for when first coming here and seeking work?

(PJ) Frankly, be prepared to struggle a bit. NYC is a tough place and it's harder now than when I first moved here because of the rising rents. Subsidized housing is one option to look into. Get to know other musicians and play as much as possible so that your playing can be heard, even if it's not a paying gig. Someone might hear you, like your playing and offer you a paying gig. Try and get along with people. Some individuals can be difficult to work with so try and give them a reasonable amount of slack, but not to the point where you get abused. Take example from Frank Sinatra and "don't take any shit from people."

Being able to read music is a definite asset. A lot of players play with several bands and have to be on top of a lot of material. I don't sight read notation since I never formally studied music so I rely on my memory as much as possible. Being able to read and having a good memory is a great combination. Putting a lot of feeling into your playing goes without saying, which is something that probably can't be taught anyway.

Be organized, especially if you are playing in several bands, and try not to bail out of gigs at short notice. A bandleader might not use you again if you let him down too often, even though he might think highly of your playing.

(JC) You are one of the most revered and innovative fretless bass players. Who are some of your influences and what bassists or musicians have inspired you over the years?

(PJ) I started playing bass in the early 60s. The electric bass was a relatively new instrument at that point and there weren't many players who had an advanced technique back then. One exception was Cliff Barton who played with Georgie Fame and The Blue Flames. He unfortunately passed away in his mid 20s. I mostly listened to upright players for inspiration. Some examples are Scott LaFaro, Jimmy Garrison and Charles Mingus. Mingus I think is an overall favorite, not just on account of his bass playing but his unpredictable compositional style also. Of the more contemporary upright players I like Miroslav Vitous's work. Renaud Garcia Fons is a very good, relatively new player.

As for electric bass players, there are tons of good players out there. I tend to like players who have a true bass sensibility and play like bass players as opposed to guitar players; some examples are James Jamerson, Michael Henderson and Anthony Jackson. I also like the more contemporary guys such as Michael Manring, Matt Garrison, Gary Willis and Laurence Cottle, just to name a few.

(JC) Can you discuss the gear you're currently using?

(PJ) My bass is a wooden version of the Ibanez Ergodyne with some extra mods. I had tried the original Ergodyne which had a plastic body and found it had a rather interesting sound just using the piezo pickups. It had a huge dynamic range but was very unstable in changing weather conditions and had a rather brittle response. I asked Ibanez it they would make a wooden version with a Mahogany body and a thicker more rigid neck. They came up with a nice bass that was a substantial improvement. The sound was warmer and the neck was very stable. Also the pickups were better and I think the preamp had also been modified. The original bass had an annoying resonance up around 11 KHz which is absent in the new bass. They also later added a string tree to stop the short length of string between the nut and machine heads from ringing. It's a rather challenging bass to play because the piezos pick up everything; string squeak is something I always have to watch, but the dynamic range is great and I can get a lot of variation in dynamics just from my hands. I wanted to try another direction from magnetic pickups. It's still a work in progress.

Regarding amplifiers, it got to the point where I had to start using something smaller that would fit into a small van with all the other Tunnels gear. I went out and bought an SWR Workingman's combo. I used it for a while but was frustrated by the power compression and lack of headroom. It was really frustrating after using the bi-amped 18" and 2X10" that I had used previously. I then looked around for bass amps using transmission line cabinets. These designs more efficiently match the speaker acoustic impedance to the impedance of the open air. Euphonic Audio seemed to be the only manufacturer that I could find. I ended up getting an iamp 800 combo. It has a very potent class D power amp and a 12" speaker in a transmission line cabinet. It's surprisingly loud and clean sounding for its size.

www.MySpace.com/TheMusicOfTunnels
www.PercyJones.net

Bassist: Percy Jones
Interviewed by: John Carey

www.JohnCarey.net

Interview with NYC bassist, Nicholas D'Amato:

Nicholas D'Amato is currently working with Lizz Wright to promote her new release, *The Orchard* (Verve), as well as performing with NYC Indie sensations, Pete and J. He keeps a busy recording schedule recording albums and tracks for some of NY's finest, as well as television jingles and film scores. Nicholas has toured the world with contemporary blues heavyweight, Popa Chubby. In 2006, he released his own record, *Nullius In Verba* (Buckyball). He has also worked with Wayne Krantz, Dave Binney and singer-songwriter, Janita.

(JC) How long have you been involved in the New York City music scene, and how have you seen it change over the years, with regard to bass related work?

(ND) I started playing in the scene in 1996, playing with bands and trying to figure out what it meant to be a "freelance bassist." But I kind of consider 2000 the year I really started giving it my all. That's when I stopped doing any part time day jobs and I really took the leap of faith that is required to crack this nut. I've seen a lot of changes since I've been here, and a lot has stayed the same. I was lucky to have a chance to experience some of the tail end of the studio days. In the late 90s, I was going to swanky jingle houses to do commercials and some film scores. A remarkable amount of the commercials were "finals" but I was so naive, I didn't know how lucky that was. As the residual checks dried up and the calls stopped coming, I was glad I got to have even a little taste of that scene. It was a cool challenge and fun to hear yourself on TV. I still do some records for a few producers who use me, but largely it's all home-based stuff now. As far as changes to the live scene, I think I was on the road when it was at a low point, 2002-2006. I remember coming home and hearing other bassists talk about there being a lot less work. But I think it's come back around these last few years. There's an influx of killing young players with a lot of energy and talent, and it is fun to work with them. There seems to be no end of small gigs to play around town. Myspace has been a huge change. You can meet someone one night after they played a really quiet singer/songwriter gig, and go home to check out their Myspace to discover that their great passion is Balkan death metal. It allows people to really express and sell themselves to a broader audience. As a freelancer, it is my permanent business card that allows people to hear a really wide range of what I can do, all in one place. I think NYC is pretty healthy at the moment. I worry about the economy slowing things down. I'm lucky to be on the road a lot lately, but I would be scared if my only income was songwriters who need a bass player for set at Rockwood, where they play for tips, and they somehow have to come up with $2000 a month for rent. But the good ones always seem to do it!

(JC) If you had to choose five attributes (musically or personally) that a bass player must have in order to be a working bassist here in New York, what would they be?

(ND)
1. Resilience. To stay at it is the key. It sounds trite but this place will kick you, and you will have bad nights and you will struggle to pay the bills. But if you simply do not even allow the notion of failure to enter into your equation, you can keep bouncing back.
2. Honesty. Be honest with yourself, to accurately assess your strengths and weaknesses both as a player and as a person, and be honest with those with whom you work. Do the right thing and don't let money ruin things.
3. Creativity. You will need to be creative as a player, to carve out a voice on your instrument. And you will need to be creative as an individual, because we don't walk through the "normal" world.

We have to make things work without the framework of a typical job on which to hang things.
4. Friendly/Sincere. It's an incredibly small scene and there is nothing to be gained by vibing people, except those that totally deserve to be vibed, that is. But that's only because *they* are not friendly and sincere! You have to understand that with so many great players, more often than not, it comes down to you as a person. Do you want to be on a bus with yourself?
5. Be Artistic. To live artistically "informs" everything. Find magic in what you get to do. Think metaphorically. Find relationships between the most disparate seeming things and let that inform your playing.

(JC) What bass players inspire you here in New York?

(ND) There are so many! I guess "Papa Bear" for me is Will Lee. He plays everything with such intensity and focus. I saw him at the 55 Bar, playing to thirty or so people, jumping up and down driving the shit of the band. Inspiration! I respect so many people in this town. Tim Lefebvre has always inspired me. I think of Richard Hammond and Rob Calder so often when I play. Anthony Jackson defines some aspects of NYC bass for me. Actually, so does Reggie Washington. Although technically not a NY bass player right now, Michael Formanek was and is still a HUGE influence. I studied with him for five years and took so many lessons from him that I'm still sorting through them years later. He just embodies the roll of the instrument to me . . . the sound, the time, the push and pull of duties within a group. Everything.

(JC) How important is developing one's "image," for bassists and sidemen in general? And what other business oriented (non-musical) tips might you give players?

(ND) I think it's silly to deny that image is not important. I'm a raging idealist and I would love to say that the music is all that matters, but I can't. You are a product and you are selling your own "brand." The most important thing is the quality of the product: you can play, you are on time and you are open and receptive. But like all products, you've got to choose some packaging. This includes your dress, for sure, but it also includes your attitude. Don't show up with a wildly inappropriate bass just because you want to prove something, whether it be with nine strings or two strings. You are a brand and you want people to trust the product you have spent years developing. Be adaptable to a point, but stay true to your brand's core attributes. Realize that rarely can one product be all things to all people. Your image can change with time, but find those things that you do naturally, bring them to the surface and let people come to your brand. Then the whole question of "image" is moot . . . you're just you.

(JC) What are some of your favorite NYC venues to play at and why?

(ND) I love playing at Rockwood. Ken is so sincere and his tastes are so varied. He always does a great job making it sound beautiful and then stays out of the way of the music. I recently started to like The Living Room. I've been doing a residency there for months with Pete & J, and I've come to trust the sound. It can be a bit "scene-y," but hell, that's life. I love the Highline Ballroom . . . Great stage sound and nice vibe.

Actually, I don't really like too many NYC venues! I wish an "innocent until proven guilty" system towards the artists could take hold regarding the soundmen for shows; why won't a soundman just smile and be friendly before the set? If we suck, or act like jerks, then by all means, be a prick after the show!

www.NicholasDAmato.com

Bassist: Nicholas D'Amato
Interviewed by: John Carey

www.JohnCarey.net

Photo by Karen Tweedy-Holmes

Interview with NYC bassist, Dave Hofstra:

Dave Hofstra plays acoustic bass, tuba, bass saxophone and Fender bass. He lives in New York City. Dave has played with artists such as Elliot Sharp, Bill Frisell, Rachelle Garniez, Dave Sewelson, Joe Ruddick, John Zorn, Metropolitan Klezmer, Marc Ribot, Bobby Previte, Lou Grassi, Bobby Radcliff, Otis Rush, Earl King, Hubert Sumlin, Thunderbird Davis, Grady Gaines, Wayne Horvitz, Robin Holcomb, Guy Klucevsek, Joel Forrester, William Parker, Claire Daly, Marshall Crenshaw and Nora York, as well as with Phillip Johnston's Big Trouble, the Microscopic Septet, The Waitresses and Sleepy LaBeef, to name a few.

(JC) When did you enter the music scene here in New York City and what were your initial impressions? What were some of the first gigs you got and how did you originally go about seeking work?

(DH) I came to NYC in 1976. The first person I saw play was Walter Davis Jr., with Alex Blake on bass, and I almost turned around and went home. I've always just played with whoever called me. Some of the first people I worked with were Phillip Johnston, Jody Harris, Bob Musial, Charles Carrington and Keith Lawrence.

(JC) Since you have been here in New York, how have you witnessed the music scene change?

(DH) It's gotten louder. There seem to be fewer clubs, and checker cabs have disappeared.

(JC) If you could only choose five attributes (musically or personally) that a bassist must have in order to be a successful player here in New York, what would they be?

(DH) There are only three:
1. Show up on time.
2. Deliver the part.
3. Keep your mouth shut.

(JC) When you first entered the scene here, were there any bassists that you looked to for advice (musically or music business related)? What players inspired you when you were new to the scene?

(DH) I learned a great deal from Marshall Brown, who was mostly known as a trombonist, but also played bass.

(JC) Is there any advice you can give to bass players considering relocating to New York with hopes of playing bass for a living?

(DH) Bring a black suit and a white shirt.

Bassist: Dave Hofstra
Interviewed by: John Carey

www.JohnCarey.net

Interview with NYC bassist, Leo Traversa:

Leo Traversa is a professional bassist, clinician, bass educator and author located in New York City for over twenty years. He has worked with Tania Maria, Randy Brecker, Ben E. King, Astrud Gilberto, Michael Brecker, Don Byron, Cesar Camargo Mariano, Claudio Roditi, DaveValentin, Toninho Horta, Gerry Mulligan, The New York Voices, Oscar Hernandez, Phil Woods, Dianne Reeves, Milton Nascimento, Fantcha, Bebel Gilberto, Eileen Ivers, The Caribbean Jazz Project, Herbie Mann, Kenia, Shoko Aida, Aster Aweke, Louis Bellson, Steve Kimock, Dave Kikoski, Gato Barbieri and Ivan Lins to name but a few. In addition, Leo has worked extensively on Broadway, and in film and TV.

Leo is a graduate of the Berklee College of Music in Boston, MA. He is a founding member of the Bass Collective, NYC and is also on staff there as an active faculty member. He is author of, *Fusion: A Study of Contemporary Music for the Bass* and *Afro Caribbean and Brazilian Rhythms for the Bass, The Collective Series*, published by Carl Fischer.

(JC) When did you enter the New York City music scene, and what were your initial impressions? What were some of the first gigs you picked up and how did you go about seeking work at the time?

(LT) I moved to the city in 1984 after going to school in Boston. Since I was working a lot in Boston at the time, I moved gradually, coming to NYC during the week and going back to Boston to work on weekends. My first impressions were great. There seemed to be so many more opportunities, and I already had a lot of friends here from school and from home.

When I made the final move, I worked as a bicycle messenger until I could get enough gigs. Thankfully, that only took a couple of months. In my early days in NYC, I would just do anything that anyone called me to do. A lot of ten dollar gigs, covering rehearsals for guys, demo sessions (for those who remember the days before you could record your music at home and actually had to go to a recording studio and hire other musicians.) Doing those low budget gigs and helping guys out with rehearsals turned out to be very helpful in establishing myself and led directly to future work.

(JC) How would you describe the bass community here in New York City in its current state? Also, how have you witnessed the music scene change over the twenty years you've been working here?

(LT) The bass community here is incredible, thanks in part to guys like you and Mike Visceglia who do things like this book of interviews and the NYC bass brunch. It seems to me that here in NYC the bass community is tight and supportive. We all have our pages of bass player's numbers in our books that we call and share work with or call and beg to bail us out of a tight spot. It's funny how sometimes you can know a fellow bass player for years through telephone calls but don't actually meet until ten years later. Since we don't play on the bandstand together, it's only at events like the bass brunch or festivals where we get to meet and hang. The faculty meetings at the Bass Collective are kind of like that. So was a

Larry Graham concert I saw years ago at Tramps. Every bass player in NYC was there.

Speaking of Tramps, that leads into the next question about change. It seems like there aren't as many places to play live as there was when I came to town. In the 80s, I could see Marcus, Will, Anthony or Jaco just about any night of the week . . . for five or ten bucks, or for free. There were more venues available to musicians to play live and get paid at the end of the night. Another change is that there is less recording work. With the technology we have now, musicians can do a lot of work by themselves that couldn't be done as well in the 80s and early 90s. So, for me, there was more recording work in my early years here. I'd be interested to see what some of the other guys say about that.

(JC) What attributes do you believe bassists must have (musically or personally) in order to be working bassists here in NYC?

(LT) First, and obvious, is a level of skill and competence that allows you to perform the music you are playing. I think you should either be really great at one style or be very versatile and capable of playing many styles of music. The more you know, the more opportunities you have. Reading is a good skill to have if you plan on doing recording sessions or shows. Good reading ability also allows you to sub for guys and come in and do gigs at the last minute without rehearsal, which you'll find happens quite often in NYC. Being reliable and professional is crucial. Showing up on time with good gear and a good sound is a great way to endear yourself to any potential employers and show them that you know how to take care of business. As far as personal traits, you should be able to listen to instructions, accept criticism or praise gracefully and get along with people. Don't put yourself ahead of anyone, even if their skill level is below yours. Learn how to speak to people respectfully and diplomatically if you have suggestions or criticism. And it's probably a good idea to learn how to travel well. Be a "low maintenance" traveler.

(JC) Do you feel that a formal music education is mandatory to be a working bassist in NYC?

(LT) I wouldn't say it's mandatory. It all depends on what you want to do with your career. For me, I like so many different kinds of music from around the world so my education helped me to learn and absorb things faster. Also, by going to college, I was able to meet musicians from around the world that were an influence on my career. So, if you want to play a lot of different music in a lot of different situations, an education is important.

Many musicians are capable of having great careers without formal education. If you specialize in one kind of music or play original music only, you can be successful without a formal education.

(JC) What do you see yourself doing twenty-five years from now? Would you like to remain in NYC? What do you think your main focus might be musically?

(LT) I think I'll always have a place in NYC. I'm a native so this is home for me but honestly, in twenty-five years, I see myself scuba diving in Bonaire or sipping an espresso somewhere in Italy.

www.MySpace.com/LeoTraversa
www.LeoTraversa.com

Bassist: Leo Traversa
Interviewed by: John Carey

www.JohnCarey.net

Photo by Kevin McIntyre

Interview with NYC bassist, Richard Hammond:

Richard Hammond is a professional acoustic and electric bassist, composer, producer and author living in New York City. Originally from New Zealand, Richard moved to the States at age twenty-two. Richard earned a Bachelor's Degree in Performance on Acoustic Bass at Berklee College of Music and went on to attend Manhattan School of Music, where he earned a Master's Degree in Jazz/Commercial music. Richard has worked with Joan Osborne, Erasure, The East Village Opera Company, Angelique Kidjo, Jonatha Brooke, Carlos Santana, Gavin DeGraw, Dar Williams, Chiara Civello, Shannon McNally, Louis Bellson and Jim Campilongo to name a few. In addition, he has also recorded on several major motion picture soundtracks, and he has worked as composer/producer on several national advertising campaigns. Richard is co-author of *Teach Yourself Visually Bass Guitar* (Wiley Publishing), and has worked as an instructor for the National Guitar Workshop, and as a clinician for Berklee College of Music.

(JC) At what age did you enter the New York City music scene, and what were your initial impressions? What were some of your first gigs and how did you go about seeking work when you arrived?

(RH) When I first arrived in NYC, I was twenty-eight and attending Manhattan School of Music, studying for my graduate degree in Jazz. I had just finished my undergrad degree at Berklee College of Music, and I was shuttling back and forth to Boston each weekend scraping together whatever gigs I could to get by. So with that and the mountain of stuff I had to get done for my studies, there was very little time to get out and be a part of the scene . . . frustrating to say the least. Once I was done with all the schooling, I basically headed down to the Village and hung out around the Bitter End and some of the other clubs still standing. I caught the tail end of the West Village heyday, and found myself working most nights doing whatever came my way . . . lots of singer songwriter gigs, the Mann-made Jam session, and a lot of the graveyard shift gigs at the Bitter End. I was also doing a fair amount of club date work, thanks to Jon Albrink (great bassist/singer-songwriter), who I will never stop thanking, as he was primarily responsible for me being able to feed myself that year. I think I got work in the West Village scene by being as visible as possible in the place where there was the biggest amount of musicians passing through, and playing with whomever, whenever, and doing all the jamming that I could. Once the work was flowing in more regularly, I was able to be a little more selective. I was also surrounded by a great network of friends from Boston that had also relocated, so there was a bonafide community that I was part of. We all found ourselves in different combinations backing up all kinds of different artists over that time period.

(JC) How have you seen the state of the music business change since you moved here, specifically with regard to getting work as a sideman?

(RH) In the broader sense, the music business has undergone and is still undergoing massive change in terms of label structure and the advent of downloading and it's effect on the record biz. In terms of the New York microcosm, it's the same old thing: clubs come, clubs go; scenes dry up in one location and start up somewhere else. That's what I love about this town. It's hugely dynamic and constantly reinventing itself. In terms of getting work as a sideman, that's a difficult thing to answer in general terms as it is so case specific. Everyone's career trajectory ebbs and flows in different ways determined by the choices they make. As you move up the ladder, the nature of the work changes, and so the do the kind of choices you have to make regarding that work. The one thing I can say is that jingle work seems to be thinner on the ground these days. Advertising music budgets have shrunk dramatically, and so in order for the larger houses to stay profitable they have to rely less and less on studio musicians.

(JC) What advice can you give to those bassists here in New York looking for work with higher profile artists?

(RH) I don't really have any one answer for that. Anything that's happened for me in the past has been a case of "stars aligning" to a great degree. Enough people mentioning my name at the same time with reference to a gig. If I were to break it down, I'd say it's a cumulative thing. If you do well again and again, your rep grows and you find yourself on more and more folk's radars.

(JC) What five attributes (musically or personally) must a bassist have, in your opinion, in order to get and maintain work here in NYC?

(RH)
1. Be together. Be cool, and easy to work with and give a good hang. Make people comfortable to be around you. Have the basics squarely taken care of.
2. Be together musically. Know what it means to be a bass player, and understand the profundity of playing "time" and having a groove.
3. Be together stylistically. Whatever style or styles of music you choose to make your living from, make sure you fully understand that music top to bottom. Figure out what is considered currency in that world, and master the basics. Build on that from the bottom up. Speak the language fluently.
4. Be utterly prepared, all the time. Know the music you're being hired to play through and through. Aim to make whoever you play with feel that you've been playing their music all your life, and that you're really bringing something to the music.

5. Be totally present and focused. Give your all whenever you play: performance, rehearsal, basically whenever you pick up the axe. And make sure to have fun at the same time.

(JC) Do you feel that a formal education is necessary in order to be a successful working bassist in New York?

(RH) Not at all. Having a formal education is definitely valuable and I'm glad I did it, but it's just one route. Most of my favorite bassists didn't go that route. The most important thing is giving yourself the most thorough education in music, period. Learn all you can from wherever you can, and don't stop learning. If there are gaps in your education that are holding you up, fill the gaps. Go to school, get lessons, see the guys you admire play live, just learn.

www.MySpace.com/RichardHammondBass
www.Richard-Hammond.com

Bassist: Richard Hammond
Interviewed by: John Carey

www.JohnCarey.net

Interview with NYC bassist, John Conte:

John Conte is a professional bassist in New York City working extensively live, in the studio, and with commercial and TV work. He has worked with Phil Ramone, Levon Helm, Tony Visconti, David Bowie, Joan Osborne, Billy Joel, Gavin DeGraw, Southside Johnny and Rachael Yamagata to name a few. He has also played bass for the Broadway production, *Movin' Out*. John has been heard on countless jingles.

(JC) What advice can you give to bassists in NYC who are already competent players but are seeking work with higher profile artists?

(Conte) Well, it's not like if you're an actor and you can open up "Variety Magazine" and see ads for open call auditions. I personally don't know of anything like that in existence for musicians. But heck, don't take my word for it. Perhaps there is some website for that sort of thing now. One should certainly be as resourceful as they can.

All of my work with "higher profile" artists has come by word of mouth, mutual acquaintances and recommendations. There have been instances when I heard that an artist was auditioning bass players. In those situations, I had known someone connected to that artist, so I called them and asked for the management's contact info and also asked if I could use their name as a reference.

It's very difficult to deal with people in the music business on that level without a mutual connection or reference. That can be a big key to things. We've all heard the tired old expression "it's who you know." But there *is* some truth to it. So, I guess the question is: How do you make those connections?

While the artist themselves may not be accessible to you, it's likely that the players in their band may be more accessible to you. If you don't happen to know any of these players personally find out who they are. (It's certainly easier than ever to find out anything these days via the Internet if all else fails.) If you're from NYC and the players you're looking to connect with are in NYC then of course the whole prospect is more plausible. See if you can catch them when they're off of the road and they're doing their own gig in town or backing a local artist. Approach this person after the show and introduce yourself. Tell them that you like their work and mention a little bit about yourself. Keep it short and simple. Certainly if you have any mutual acquaintances you can mention that. This may sound sort of elementary, but if you want to be proactive it's one of the best suggestions I can think of. You've got to start somewhere. If you keep seeing this person around on the scene and you become a familiar face to them, you can more comfortably invite them to one of your own gigs so they can hear what *you* do. You could eventually even hire them for a gig or a session that you are putting together. If you're confident about your abilities as a player, then you've got nothing to lose. If you've got the goods you just need to make the right relationships with other players, producers, artists and managers.

(JC) When did you first begin to work in NYC as a bassist, and how would you describe the music scene then? What were some of your first gigs here and how did you go about getting them?

(Conte) I started working in NYC in the fall of 1985, after I finished college. I had taken my first road gig with Blood Sweat & Tears (featuring David Clayton Thomas) to get some touring experience, but I was hanging out in NYC whenever I could to start making myself visible because I knew this is where I wanted to be. One of the first things I remember is a Monday night jam session at Kenny's Castaways on Bleeker Street (sometimes hosted by Frank Gravis) where I initially met a bunch of working cats. I ended up working with a bunch of the people that I met down there like guitarists Jon Paris and Jeff Golub. I also met singer/songwriters from the Bleecker St. scene, and started playing on song demos for fifty bucks a pop. I tried to do as much recording as possible no matter how little it paid, in order to gain the experience of putting my playing under the microscope while meeting the people behind the scenes doing this work . . . the producers, engineers and writers.

Through my brother Steve (guitarist, singer and songwriter), I ended up playing with a singer named Robin Beck, a pretty successful backup vocalist at the time. She had toured with David Bowie and was singing on a lot of sessions and jingles. She was pursuing a solo career and her producer was a songwriter by the name of Jeff Kent (an original member of the band Dreams with Billy Cobham, Will Lee and the Brecker Brothers). We didn't end up doing much with Robin Beck, but getting involved in the project turned out to be a good thing.

My brother and I also had this blues band called The Hudson River Rats which we formed in New Jersey with the amazing Rob Paparozzi on harmonica. Jeff Kent, who also wrote and produced a lot of jingles, needed a bluesy backing band for a commercial with blues legend, James Cotton. We ended up getting the call. Jeff loved the band and ended up promoting us at a weekly gig/jam session featuring the River Rats as the house band. It turned into a really big scene for about a year and a half; NBC even did a little feature on it for the local NYC news broadcast. Word spread and many of the other writers and producers from the NYC jingle scene came down to dust off their guitars so to speak and jump up and play with us. That's how I initially fell into the whole jingle/studio scene (many thanks Jeff!). Other celebs and musicians on tour passing through NYC would come by to sit in. I remember playing with Cyndi Lauper, Julian Lennon, Willie Deville and Carol King.

Shortly after that, my brother Steve and I met a singer, Kyf Brewer, who was doing a lot of sessions. To make long story short, we started writing songs together; Kyf brought in veteran rock drummer (and A&R guy) Frankie Larocka, and we formed a band called Company of Wolves. After a big NYC showcase gig for a number of major record labels, we were signed to a pretty big deal with Mercury/Polygram in 1989. Our first record was released in 1990 and we enjoyed some moderate success with it, scoring a few top 20 AOR tracks and touring the country for most of the year.

One day when we were in the studio with Company of Wolves, I met guitarist, vocalist and arranger Jimmy Vivino (now of *Late Night with Conan O'Brien's* band) who was also working on a session in another room. A couple years later after Company of Wolves split up, I started doing a lot of blues gigs and pickup R&B gigs with Jimmy including subbing for Harvey Brooks in The Little Big Band (which went on to be the band for Donald Fagan's original *Come Back* project, *The New York Rock n' Soul Revue*). Through Jimmy I have met a whole bunch of fabulous musicians, singers and legendary personalities. Jimmy and I continue to work together to this day.

The whole point of all this, as many other players will attest to, is that you never know where a gig will end up taking you . . . it will no doubt end up leading to something else.

(JC) How have you witnessed the music scene change in NYC?

(Conte) When I was first starting out here it seemed like there were a lot more down and dirty, unassuming type clubs to play in; places that featured blues, soul music and rock n' roll. You could just show up and play three sets of jazz standards or classic soul with a minimum of rehearsal if any, have a real good time, and make some cash. It was a great way to hone your skills and build your strength and stamina, playing three or four sets a night.

I never saw it as a long term way to make a living, but back in the mid eighties to nineties there were a lot of cats making a major chunk of their income this way. If you worked five nights a week making seventy-five to a hundred bucks a night (back when NYC rents weren't as outrageous as they are now), it was a viable way for a player to make a living by just going out and playing your instrument.

But, today if you are a young player just starting out in NYC, I don't think that you could go out and do the kind of thing that I just mentioned or do it as easily. Most of the blues and jazz clubs are gone. With gentrification, the huge construction boom and rising real estate prices, most of the "unassuming" type clubs have given way to the "trendy and swanky type" clubs where the emphasis is *not* on making a comfortable and fertile environment for live music and musicians.

But with that said, I think that there are still plenty of clubs where you can play original music, whether it's your own music or backing another artist. In fact, due to the many changes in the music and recording industry in the past decade (i.e. the indie music scene, indie labels, the Internet and computer based recording technology), it may be the best time ever to be an artist doing your own thing here in NYC, or to be a sideman backing original artists.

The other major change that I have felt is in the studio scene, especially the jingle business. Although I just sort of "fell" into the jingle business and was in the right place at the right time, it became a major source of work for me for well over a decade, and I was even doing some writing and arrangements. The biggest change in that business is the recent trend of advertising agencies licensing preexisting music, rather than hiring composers and music houses to write music for a client's ad campaign. Also, many song placement companies are springing up on the Internet. As a result, there has been less demand for original music to be written for commercials and hence, with less music being written, there are fewer sessions taking place and less session players needed. Many of the music houses I had worked for don't exist anymore, have downsized or are doing post production services. Doing recording sessions with a live band or rhythm section in a real recording studio used to be the norm. But these days that doesn't happen as often, and it's more common to be laying down your bass track in front of a computer screen with a producer or ProTools engineer in some dude's apartment. The standard used to be: learn the song, get comfortable with it and then go for a complete take. Now we're in a ProTools world and some one might just ask me to play the verse a few times, then the chorus and then the bridge. Whoever is in charge of the session ends up deciding what pieces will be on the track.

There are two ways to look at this. You could say that it compromises the integrity or intent of the player, but you could also use the technology to your advantage. Since no one is concerned about rewinding tape and wasting tracks anymore, it's easier to assert yourself and say, "hey, let's just try a completely different approach on this take" or, "let's hear what this sounds like just for shits and giggles." And sometimes when you're just having fun, that's the shit that you end up digging the most!

(JC) Who are some of your favorite NYC bassists?

(Conte) I've always liked Andy Hess for his warm traditional Fender bass tone and his commitment to the groove. He's done a lot of great gigs and he's very humble about it. One of my favorite upright players in town is Chip Jackson. He's a beautiful cat who I've known for many years as well. He makes me laugh when I see him play; he's got a lot of humor in his playing without being "cheesy." He's also got impeccable time, intonation and an effortless facility on the instrument. I've seen him pull off things on the upright that I wouldn't attempt on electric bass! He also does a lot of duo and trio gigs without a drummer and swings *so* hard. Paul Nowinski is another guy that I like on upright for his sheer command of the instrument and his voice as a soloist. Another great upright and electric player I like is Tony Garnier. He's got a lot of depth, and he seems just as comfortable with rootsy music like blues and country as with pop and jazz. I also love the fact that he plays a Rickenbacker 4001, as I do. (There are not a whole lot of us out there!) There's this guy Byron Issacs. I haven't heard a lot of him but what I've heard I really dig. I heard him with the band Ollabelle and on Levon Helm's latest CD. He's got that gift of beautiful understatement in his playing, a great feel, good note choices and a nice warm tone on upright and electric. He plays an early fifties P-bass. Jack Daley is a guy that I've always admired and that I know pretty well. We have a lot of the same influences on electric bass (McCartney, Jamerson, John Paul Jones, Dee Murray). He always plays right for the song while still putting a lot of personality and vibe into it with an earthy feel. His bass sound always seems to cut through nicely. I think he's real savvy about his gear which is a big plus. I like his pick playing too, which is something I also like to do that you don't hear too much of in town. Some other players I'd like to mention are Richard Hammond, Frank Gravis, Jerry Barnes, Bernie Menossa, Will Lee and Chris Wood.

(JC) What attributes (musically or personally) do you feel a bassist must have in order to be successful and busy in New York?

(Conte) I'll start by saying I feel that it's really important to develop your own voice on your instrument and have somewhat of a unique approach to some aspect of bass playing. Whether it's your tone, how you feel eighth notes, how you swing, the kind of gear that you use, how you play a ballad or how you react to other players. I'm feeling that it's more important these days to really find a couple of things that you do . . . that you are passionate about . . . that can define you as a player artistically, and exploit and promote those attributes or styles of playing, rather than trying to be "everything for everybody." While it doesn't hurt to be versatile, finding a niche for yourself is a worthy pursuit. This is especially important in the recording world, where a producer, songwriter or other instrumentalist can pick up a three hundred dollar bass, plug it into ProTools and dice it and slice it and then change the sound to their liking for days with dozens of plug-ins; you've got to think about bringing something more exceptional to the table. Unfortunately there will always be some people in the business that will marginalize the role of being a bass player . . . like it's the easiest thing to figure out how to do, so they may as well cut some costs and play the bass part themselves or use some samples. But I think that there are still enough producers, composers and artists in the business that value the subtleties and expertise of someone who approaches bass playing as an art.

www.JohnConteBass.com

Bassist: John Conte
Interviewed by: John Carey

www.JohnCarey.net

25 *Tips for Success*

- Get out there and network. Meet as many players and artists as possible; introduce yourself!

- Study with those who are working bassists in NYC. Take a lesson with them and pick their brain.

- Get a website. Include a biography describing your experience and schooling (if any), post MP3s of your playing, add photos and provide your contact information. Have some business cards made up as well.

- Be able to play multiple instruments. You will have an edge over other bassists if you can play guitar, piano or sing, etc.

- Own Precision and Jazz style basses. Even if boutique basses are your thing, producers, musicians and artists will most likely want to work with the more traditional and recognizable basses.

- Pick up some students and teach lessons to supplement your income. You can learn a lot from teaching others, as well as reinforce what you already know.

- Check out Craigslist.org and *The Village Voice* paper and online site. These resources can be helpful in providing you with bands in need of bassists and you can meet likeminded musicians. You can also find apartments for rent and enjoy reading the romance sections!

- Exercise. Stay fit so when you get called for that tour you can bounce back and handle the wear and tear that the road can sometimes cause. In addition, remember that image *does* count.

- Keep a positive attitude. You never know what band you work with will be successful down the road, and you never know what musicians you'll meet while working (in the band or in the audience).

- Watch engineers and producers while they work. Learn from them ... make it a goal to learn some engineering and production skills.

- Put your own project together. This will give you a chance to showcase yourself, play the music that you enjoy and perhaps make some extra money as well.

- Stay and hang for a while after your gigs. Thank people for coming down (even if it's not your own band). This is how you will meet people.

- Work on your music reading skills. Even if you do not want a Broadway gig, being able to read will help you get more familiar with your instrument. In addition, it is important to be able to write out what you play. Remember, no matter what style of music you play, you *will* be asked to read.

- You must be able to play through chord charts fluidly if you want to be a working bassist in NYC.

- Be dependable. Show up on time, respond to emails and phone calls quickly. If another player gets back in touch with an artist before you do, you might lose the opportunity.

- Have good communication and inter-personal skills. Keep an open line of communication with the artist, manager, producer, etc. Make sure they are happy and that you address their needs and concerns.

- Take some business classes or read some business related books. Remember this is the music *business* you are aspiring to be a part of. Most musicians are lacking important business skills and are unable to handle their craft as a business.

- If you are solely an electric bass player, pick up an upright bass. And vice versa! It will only strengthen your playing and will provide you with more gigging opportunities.

- Remaining in the NYC scene is perhaps the number one means to success. Do whatever it takes so that you can remain visible in the scene . . . get a flexible day job, work a wedding band, teach lessons, etc. The longer you are here, the more opportunities will come your way and more players will know about you and what you can bring to the table as a musician.

- Know some other things besides music . . . diversify. Artists don't always want to hear about the musical inner workings of their material. Be a well rounded individual, be easy to talk to, and make the artist look forward to seeing you again (as a person, as well as a musician).

- Be prepared to struggle to make ends meet for a while. You have to be the type of person that wants it so badly that you're willing to live in an apartment that might be substandard compared to what you're used to. You just might have to live off of mac and cheese for a year before you can have a well balanced meal. How badly do you want it?

- Don't get networking confused with getting entirely caught up in the scene. You're out to make contacts and further your career as a musician, not to get drunk or high. "Sex, drugs and rock and roll" will only shorten the time you will be successful in NYC. Be a professional.

- When you play, make it look easy, have fun and entertain people.

- Be aware that you *can* be a full time working bassist in NYC that only plays one or two genres of music. You can either be known as a player who "specializes," or you can be known as someone who plays several genres well. Both types of musicians can thrive in NYC. Make a conscious decision early on which avenue you'd like to take.

- Stay organized. Keep your contact list of musicians together. If you get a business card, enter it immediately into your database. Be sure to enter name (first and last), contact number, email address and any website information.

New York City Wisdom, Perspective and Inspiration (extracted from interview section)

"It takes a lot of self control and realizing that 99.9% of all gigs are not about you. The sooner you learn that in New York the sooner you'll be making a living here."
—***Chris Tarry***

"I feel like I grow and evolve musically and personally every day that I am here even after seventeen years in the city."
—***Johannes Weidenmueller***

"You have to understand that with so many great players, more often than not, it comes down to you as a person. Do you want to be on a bus with yourself?"
—***Nicholas D'Amato***

"Good reading ability also allows you to sub for guys and come in and do gigs at the last minute without rehearsal, which you'll find happens quite often in NYC."
—***Leo Traversa***

". . . When you realize as a producer what type of bass playing makes the best sounding record, it is a bit different than the perspective of most bassists."
—***Jack Daley***

"There is always a demand for good musicianship, and those who can turn up and do the job quickly and capably will always be in demand."
—***Mark Plati***

"Years ago I realized that a singing bassist had an edge and often got hired over a non-singing player."
—***Bailey Gee***

"I try to look to everyone for guidance. There is always something to be learned from someone's experiences, be it the right or wrong way to do things."
—*Brian Killeen*

"Since I've been here, I've noticed a lot more heavy musicians embracing the stability and convenience of a Broadway gig."
—*Conrad Korsch*

"It's gotten louder. There seem to be fewer clubs, and checker cabs have disappeared."
—*Dave Hofstra*

"My survival has completely depended on my ability to remake myself and learn a new genre."
—*Frank Gravis*

"Our role as bass players is primarily a supportive one. I think we tend to be supportive of each other and that's what keeps us working."
—*Irio O'Farrill*

"Even though your goal may be Madison Square Garden, taking a $30 blues gig in an Irish bar might eventually get you that gig [at MSG]."
—*Ivan "Funkboy" Bodley*

"Being twenty years old when I arrived, I really had no idea of the scene, but soon found out that you have to pay some serious dues before you're accepted into it."
—*Janek Gwizdala*

"The question I think more about is how we need to adapt ourselves to an ever-evolving world, in terms of both diversifying our skill sets and expanding our notion of what our work should be."
—*Jeff Allen*

"You need stay focused on being creative, which is the core reason why someone decides to be a full-time musician, but realize you need to make a living."
—*Jerry McDonald*

"It is a challenge to maintain both [ability on electric and upright bass], especially since life usually isn't a music camp and reality tries hard to take you somewhere else."
—*Kim Clarke*

"The election of Mayor Giuliani and Mayor Bloomberg has killed the music industry in New York City."
—*Li'nard*

"Someone once told me that being a successful musician was 20% talent, 20% persistence and 60% luck."
—*Malcolm Gold*

"Be able to communicate with the artist and play the way they hear it."
—*Meshell Ndegéocello*

"Get your personal and professional skills in tip top shape."
—*Mike Visceglia*

"The studio work you get will come through your live gigs and contacts initially."
—*Neil Jason*

"Network … Go see good music where there will be musicians and producers hanging out where you can meet them."
—*Paul Frazier*

"Never get complacent about any success you might have. On the other hand, when things are bad, you never know what lies around the corner."
—*Percy Jones*

"If you do well again and again, your rep grows and you find yourself on more and more folk's radars."
—*Richard Hammond*

"A bass is an inanimate object— there is no inherent satisfaction that comes from making them independent of the player."
—*Roger Sadowsky*

"I have tried to teach my students to be well-rounded musicians and to be familiar with all styles of music, especially if you want to be a working musician."
—*Roy De Jesus*

". . . The worst day in the life of a professional musician is probably better than a good day at most other jobs."
—*Steve Jenkins*

"Some of the smartest people I know never went to college at all and are successful in the music biz."
—*Tim Lefebvre*

"I think bassists in general are the mediators, both musically and personally in most bands, straddling the line between rhythm and harmony, bridging all the proverbial gaps between personalities, and maintaining the calm amongst a guitar riff and drum-fill filled world."
—*John Abbey*

"You have to be open to everything, willing to listen and embrace."
—*Reggie Washington*

"If you keep seeing players around on the scene and you become a familiar face to them, you can more comfortably invite them to one of your own gigs so they can hear what you do."
—*John Conte*

Your Notes . . .